Volume 17, Number 1, 2016

Quarterly Review
OF Distance
Education

RESEARCH THAT GUIDES PRACTICE

Editors:
Michael Simonson
Charles Schlosser

IAP
INFORMATION AGE
PUBLISHING

An Official Journal of the
Association for Educational Communications and Technology

Quarterly Review of Distance Education

"Research That Guides Practice"
Volume 17 Number 1, 2016

ARTICLES

STATEMENT OF PURPOSE

The *Quarterly Review of Distance Education* is a rigorously refereed journal publishing articles, research briefs, reviews, and editorials dealing with the theories, research, and practices of distance education. The *Quarterly Review* publishes articles that utilize various methodologies that permit generalizable results which help guide the practice of the field of distance education in the public and private sectors. The *Quarterly Review* publishes full-length manuscripts as well as research briefs, editorials, reviews of programs and scholarly works, and columns. The *Quarterly Review* defines distance education as institutionally based, formal education, where the learning group is separated and where interactive technologies are used to unite the learning group.

DIRECTIONS TO CONTRIBUTORS

Submit four copies of your manuscript, typed double-spaced on 8½ × 11 paper. Manuscripts should be between 10 and 30 pages in length and must conform to the style of the *Publication Manual of the American Psychological Association* (6th ed.). Research Briefs may be shorter, normally between 3 and 10 pages.

The name(s), affiliation(s), address(es), phone numbers, e-mail address(es), and a brief biography of the author(s) should appear on a separate cover page. To ensure anonymity in the review process, names of author(s) should not appear elsewhere in the manuscript, except in appropriate citations. An abstract of 100 words should also be submitted and typed on a separate page.

Printed documents should also be submitted on a flash drive using a recent version of Microsoft Word. The drive should be clearly labeled with the author(s) name(s) and name and version of the word processing program used. Also include an RTF version of the document. Graphics should be in a separate file, clearly labeled, not included as part of the Word document.

Manuscripts will be reviewed by at least three consulting editors. This process normally takes from 3-4 months.

Submit manuscripts to:

Michael Simonson
Charles Schlosser
Editors
Department of Instructional Design and Technology
Fischler College of Education
Nova Southeastern University
1750 NE 167th Street
North Miami Beach, FL 33162
simsmich@nova.edu

Name of Publication: *Quarterly Review of Distance Education*
(ISSN: 1528-3518)
Issue: Volume 17 Number 1 2016
Frequency: Quarterly

Office of Publication: IAP–Information Age Publishing, Inc.
P.O. Box 79049
Charlotte, NC 28271-7047
Tel: 704-752-9125
Fax: 704-752-9113
E-mail: QRDE@infoagepub.com
Web Address: www.infoagepub.com

Subscription Rates:

Institutions Print: $200.00
Personal Print: $95.00
Student Print: $65.00

Single Issue Price (print only): Institutions: $45.00, Personal $25.00
Back Issue Special Price (print only): Institutions $100.00;
Personal: $50.00; Student: $35.00
Outside the U.S. please add $25.00 for surface mail.

Editorial Office: *Quarterly Review of Distance Education*
Department of Instructional Design and Technology
Fischler College of Education
Nova Southeastern University
1750 NE 167th Street
North Miami Beach, FL 33162
800-986-3223 ext. 8563
simsmich@nova.edu

Quarterly Review of Distance Education is indexed
by the DE Hub Database of Distance Education.

AN ONLINE SOCIAL CONSTRUCTIVIST COURSE
Toward a Framework for Usability Evaluations

Alana S. Phillips, Anneliese Sheffield, Michelle Moore, and Heather A. Robinson
University of North Texas

There is a need for a holistic usability evaluation framework that accommodates social constructivist online courses. Social knowledge construction may not be adequately evaluated using current frameworks. This qualitative research study examined the usability needs of a social constructivist online course. Data from an online course were analyzed using phenomenography. The data were applied to an existing framework for usability evaluations. It is recommended that usability researchers classify usability concerns as either challenge or hindrance stress in order to eliminate hindrance stress and to appropriately select and pace challenge stress. Hindrance and challenge stress identified in this study are discussed.

INTRODUCTION

Usability evaluations are important for examining the flow and effectiveness of a course environment. Although traditional usability evaluations examine aspects such as the ease of use and the look and feel of the course, it has been argued that instructional design features as well as the motivation to learn can, to a degree, be assessed using a usability evaluation framework (Zaharias, 2009). Usability concerns may be identified by the presence of user stress. In education, not all stress is considered detrimental. Some stress is helpful to learning (Joëls, Pu, Wiegert, Oitzl, & Krugers, 2006). This article examines the application of a holistic constructivist usability framework to a social constructivist course through the lens of challenge and hindrance stress. The article also offers suggestions for courses that hinge on synchronous and asynchronous interpersonal interactions.

• **Alana S. Phillips**, University of North Texas, 3940 N. Elm, Suite G150, Denton, TX 76207. Telephone: (936) 425-1223. E-mail: asp0083@unt.edu • **Anneliese Sheffield**, University of North Texas, 3940 N. Elm, Suite G150, Denton, TX 76207. Telephone: +86 158 0095 1652. E-mail: anneliesesheffield@my.unt.edu • **Michelle Moore**, University of North Texas, 3940 N. Elm, Suite G150, Denton, TX 76207. Telephone: (620) 222-7907. E-mail: mdm0413@unt.edu • **Heather A. Robinson**, University of North Texas, 3940 N. Elm, Suite G150, Denton, TX 76207. Telephone: (207) 259-0303. E-mail: har0033@unt.edu

The Quarterly Review of Distance Education, Volume 17(1), 2016, pp. 1–10
ISSN 1528-3518

OBJECTIVES

Usability evaluation is an integral part of the course design process (Cennamo & Kalk, 2005; Piskurich, 2006). However, the process of improving design through usability evaluation occurs more frequently in software and other consumer product development than in online course development (Fisher & Wright, 2010). Some usability evaluations for online courses may not appropriately address all aspects of the learners' needs. Specifically, when usability evaluation is applied to online courses, the learners' pedagogical needs are not always addressed (Zaharias & Poylymenakou, 2009).

The following research question guided the study: How can a usability evaluation framework designed for constructivist online courses be used to support the needs of social constructivist online courses? The Zaharias's (2005) usability framework for online learning informed this study. The framework combined Web design, instructional design, and Keller's (1983) motivation to learn.

THEORETICAL FRAMEWORK

Zaharias (2005, 2009) presented a usability evaluation framework for constructivist online courses with asynchronous interactions. This usability framework went beyond traditional usability evaluations to include not just usability, but constructs to measure the instructional design and motivation to learn. Within this framework, the parameters and attributes are as follows:

- *Usability*: navigation, learnability, accessibility, consistency, and visual design
- *Instructional design*: interactivity/engagement, content and resources, media use, learning strategies design, feedback, instructional assessment, and learner guidance and support
- *Motivation to learn*: attention, relevance, confidence, and satisfaction.

Zaharias referred to these as *functional connections*, *cognitive (learning) connections*, and *affective (learning) connections* (Zaharias, 2009). This holistic framework examines not only task completion but also the application of key principles of pedagogy and learning theory (Zaharias & Poylymenakou, 2009).

Zaharias (2009) offered the framework as a foundation from which to build. Alterations and adaptations were welcomed: "As Heller and Martin assert, this framework and the respective criteria can be 'the floor not a ceiling for a series of guidelines that can be used to generate evaluation questions' about an e-learning application" (Zaharias, 2009, p. 50).

In a social constructivist course, as opposed to a constructivist course, it is recommended that the usability evaluation take into consideration the social context of the course (Blandin, 2003). "A convergence appears between cognitive approaches and sociological approaches which advocates the importance of cultural and sociological context for determining 'usability' of tools, in both its restricted and broad acceptances" (Blandin, 2003, p. 317).

Social Constructivism

Social constructivism refers to the Vygotskyian version of constructivism that includes collaboration with others as a key component. The zone of proximal development (ZPD) "is the distance between the actual developmental level as determined by independent problem solving and the level of potential development as determined through problem solving under adult guidance or in collaboration with more capable peers" (Vygotsky, 1978, p. 87). At its core, the philosophy behind a social constructivist course is that knowledge is created when it is shared. "Many versions of [social constructivism] maintain that objects exist only after they enter communicative space" (Keaton & Bodie, 2011, p. 192).

Additionally, in a social constructivist course, designers and instructors do not want to tell the learners exactly what to do. Tam

(2000) explained that the constructivist perspective "summons instructional designers to make a radical shift in their thinking and to develop rich learning environments that help to translate the philosophy of constructivism into actual practice" (p. 54). Learners are often given a level of control over their own assignments while the instructor provides structure and scaffolding support (Tam, 2000). Assessment in a social constructivist course provides additional opportunities for learner involvement. Learners can work with their peers to evaluate one another's work, which is expected to help the learners foster a refined understanding of the content. This perspective means the designer and instructor relinquish some control of the course.

Usability and Stress

While in an online class and using a learning management system (LMS), students deal with both computers and communications (Brown, Fuller, & Vician, 2004), which can be challenging and contain uncertainty on their own. Individuals may experience computer anxiety, communication apprehension, or a combination of both. Brown et al. (2004) proposed that different types of computer applications may cause different types of anxiety.

Anxiety has been shown to have a positive correlation with stress (Mughal, Walsh, & Wilding, 1996). Anxiety is the concept or feeling; stress is a stimulus (Sarason, 1984). Stress can be defined as "a physical, chemical, or emotional factor that causes bodily or mental tension" (Stress, 1999, p. 1164). Low usability can be a factor in causing anxiety (stress) and impact on motivation, but not all stress is bad. Stress is considered helpful for individuals to learn (Joëls et al., 2006).

In learning, LePine, LePine, and Jackson (2004) divided stress into two categories: challenge stress and hindrance stress. Using terms from a work-related stress study, challenge stress includes "demands or circumstances that, although potentially stressful, have associated potential gains for individuals [while

hindrance stressors] tend to constrain or interfere with an individual's work achievement, and which do not tend to be associated with potential gains for the individual" (Cavanaugh, Boswell, Roehling, & Boudreau, 2000, p. 68).

Examples of challenge stress included the number of projects, the level of difficulty, and the amount of time needed to complete the work. Examples of hindrance stress included inability to understand class expectations, amount of time spent on "busy work," perceptions that favoritism rather than performance affected final grades, and unnecessary obstacles encountered before completing a project (LePine et al., 2004).

Mendoza and Novick (2005) conducted a longitudinal study of instructors as they learned to build websites and found their frustration level decreased as they progressed from novice learners to experienced users. The researchers recommended studying usability past the initial stages of a course startup. At the beginning of the study, most frustration was as a result of user error. As the course progressed, causes of frustration shifted to users having difficulty finding advanced features in the software application (Mendoza & Novick, 2005). The more they learned, the more they wanted to learn.

A social constructivist course may lend itself to fostering a certain level of frustration in users as they interact with one another and with the course to progress toward mastery. Course designers may need to identify usability items as related to either hindrance stress or challenge stress when evaluating such a course. Totally eliminating stress in a course is not desirable, as it would indicate the students are no longer learning.

PHENOMENOGRAPHY

Phenomenography is a qualitative method that is "more interested in the *content* of thinking than is traditional psychology" (Marton, 1986, p. 32), meaning the process of cognition is not as important as the meaning of the thoughts.

Phenomenography deals with people's perceptions of the world, rather than explaining the world itself. It is not based on an objectivist epistemology, but rather on a phenomenological epistemology (Sandbergh, 1997). "An effort is made to uncover all the understandings people have of specific phenomena and to sort them into conceptual categories" (Marton, 1986, p. 32). Briefly, the steps of the phenomenography method include:

- semistructured interviews or equivalent data;
- analysis of interview transcripts;
- categorization of description based on the meaning of the text; and
- analysis of categories for hierarchical relationships (Marton & Booth, 1997).

According to Marton and Booth (1997), "In principle, there is no impediment to using published documents as data, or even artifacts of other kinds that in some way serve as an expression of the ways in which people experience some part of their worlds" (p. 132).

Phenomenographic analysis of student interviews was an important addition to content analysis by an expert (McCracken, 2002). Researchers showed that students in geology courses tended to have difficulty grasping the visualization and interpretation of three-dimensional maps (Edwards, 1986). McCracken (2002) examined how the learners perceived this concept. The study found there was a disconnect between the instruction learners needed in order to adequately comprehend the material and what experts thought the learners needed; the researchers involved in the study found learners had not learned what instructors intended to teach them.

Based on these results, McCracken modified course objectives and sequencing of instruction. Results in the subsequent course offering showed an increase from pre- and posttest scores of 30% ($n = 22$), with the four students who had the lowest pretest scores showing the most gain.

METHODS AND DATA SOURCES

Study Context

This qualitative research study was designed to examine the usability evaluation needs of a social constructivist course. An online social constructivist course aimed to help teachers improve their basic online teaching and instructional design skills was selected as the context for the study.

The rich environments for active learning (REAL) instructional design model (Grabinger, Dunlap, & Duffield, 1997) guided the course design and grounded the course activities in social constructivist principles. The research argued that the REAL model supports social constructivist online instructional design (Robinson, Phillips, Moore, & Sheffield, 2014). The REAL model encourages meaningful learning through five key attributes:

- student responsibility and initiative;
- generative learning activities;
- authentic learning contexts;
- authentic assessment strategies; and
- collaborative learning (Grabinger et al., 1997).

Participants in a usability study should be real users performing real tasks (Dumas & Reddish, 1999; Genov, 2009; Rubin, 1994). "The closer that the scenarios represent reality, the more reliable the test results" (Rubin, 1994, p. 179). Participants in this course were real users. The course was designed around two major projects in which the students worked in teams to design online learning units that each team later delivered to their peers. The authentic and collaborative nature of these assignments highlights the social constructivist aspects of the course. The course content, activities, and interactions were situated largely in the Moodle LMS. Weekly synchronous meetings were also held through the web conferencing software Adobe Connect.

Rubin (1994) encouraged the use of rewards to motivate users. Motivation was a concern of the researchers because this initial offering of the course was free for volunteer participants. Attrition rates in such courses are especially high (Zaharias & Poylymenakou, 2009). Digital badges were awarded to students after the completion of certain tasks or challenges in an attempt to maintain or stimulate student motivation. These badges included metadata describing the evidence of the achievement, the skills or knowledge the learner needed in order to earn the badge, and the organization offering the badge. The badges functioned as a certification of achievement of certain benchmarks reached in the course.

Participants

Research indicated that usability testing works best when performed on four or five users (Nielson & Landauer, 1993; Virzi, 1992), for both cost and results. However, the course design called for six student teams. In order to evaluate collaboration, community building, and social knowledge construction in the course, as well as to offer a cushion against attrition, 20 class members were recruited for the online course in this study.

Faulkner (2003) offered support for larger groups of participants in qualitative usability evaluations. She challenged the use of modeling to arrive at the recommended number of four or five users. She demonstrated with users instead of models the inadequacy of that number, showing that 10 to 20 users found a higher percentage of usability problems.

The course was offered for free and without formal credits. Participants were recruited through Moodle forums, conferences, and the researchers' social networks. All participants joined the course voluntarily. Participants were aware that they were joining a newly created course and that their participation in the course's first offering would help to refine the course for future use. Participants also knew that the course and their participation in the course would be studied.

Participants in this study were adult professionals in the field of education. Some were teachers, some consultants, while others worked for educational firms. Participants ranged in experience with online learning. Some were highly experienced and had taken and taught many online courses in the past, whereas others were taking their first online course.

Data Sources

Sources of data from the course included weekly feedback from the participants, discussion forums, and activities (e.g., quizzes, surveys, and assignments). These data offered a glimpse into the natural workings of the online learning environment as well as direct comments and questions from the users about the usability of the environment.

Data Analysis

A phenomenographic approach was selected to analyze the data. The categories of description and hierarchical relationships resulting from the phenomenographic analysis were compared and contrasted with the Zaharias (2009) framework for usability evaluation. First, the data from the course were exported and compiled into a spreadsheet in preparation for coding. Utilizing a computer program to randomly determine pseudonyms, all names of students in the course were replaced with pseudonyms to anonymize the data. Then, the data were divided into thirds and coded individually by three researchers. The Zaharias framework containing 16 usability parameters was utilized as the basis for this first round of analysis. Each student question or comment was analyzed for placement into one of the 16 parameters. If stress was identified, an additional classification was applied: hindrance stress or challenge stress. These classifications comprised this first round of coding.

Finally, a second round of coding was undertaken in order to establish inter-rater agreement. The three researchers exchanged coded sections of the data. The initial codes and classifications were reviewed a second time. When disagreements arose, the researcher made comments on the codes and instances in question and suggested changes to the coding classifications as needed. Several meetings occurred during this time in which the researchers discussed various placements of categories and subcategories. This process allowed for consistency in categorical placements. The three sections of coded data were then combined for analysis of themes and categories.

RESULTS

Overall, the parameters within the cognitive (learning) connections category contained the majority of instances, specifically within the sub-parameters of interactivity, content and resources, and learning strategies design. The references and instances of both hindrance and challenge stress were highest within the learning strategies design parameter. This parameter offers a way to measure fundamental principles of learning theories and pedagogies (Zaharias, 2009). Among other things, the learning strategies design parameter allows for measurement of peer-to-peer interactions. Two of the descriptors under this parameter emphasizing peer-to-peer interactions are: (1) "The courses provide opportunities and support for learning through interaction with others (discussion or other collaborative activities)," and (2) "The courses include activities that are both individual-based and group-based" (Zaharias, 2009, p. 52).

Likely due to the social constructivist nature of the course, the peer-to-peer interactions within the learning strategies design parameter featured prominently in the data set. The course offered opportunities throughout the 16 weeks for learning through interaction with peers and the instructor with the use of discussion threads and individual activities

(asynchronous) and weekly online meetings in Adobe Connect (synchronous). Various authentic collaborative learning activities were developed for the students, including one extensive group project. Students expressed concern with:

- working across numerous time zones due to the global nature of the group (hindrance stress),
- scheduling difficulties (hindrance stress),
- team members dropping out (hindrance stress),
- inefficiencies of working collaboratively (challenge stress), and
- lack of concrete examples of projects (challenge stress).

In the course, students were allowed to self-select their groups. Instructors did not control for the time zone differences and allowed participants from around the world to enroll. The challenges that this brought to the group activity may have been a hindrance for some students to complete the course.

Some of the student statements referencing interpersonal interactions could have been classified under more than one framework classification. For example, one student described anxiety about working in a group. This statement could have been placed under learning strategies design (cognitive connection) or satisfaction (affective connection). Similarly, one student requested an earlier deadline for choosing collaborative partners. The interpersonal interaction aspect of this comment aligned with learning strategies design (cognitive connection), while the procedural side of the comment aligned well with content and resources (cognitive connection), where "content is organized in an appropriate sequence and in small modules for flexible learning" (Zaharias, 2009, p. 52). In another example, a student suggested the enabling of emoticons in the discussion forums to assist in conveying tone and intention behind comments. The interpersonal interactivity aspect of this suggestion fit in learning strategies design (cognitive connection) and, at the same time, the technical recommendation fell under visual design (functional connection).

The parameter with the second highest number of coding instances was content and resources. This parameter measures the quality of written and otherwise represented ideas in the course using "criteria such as credibility, accuracy, objectivity, coverage and currency" (Zaharias, 2009, p. 47). In this course, content was organized in weekly modules and resources were contained within online books. Learning objectives were provided for the students at the beginning of each online book. Links to readings and assignment instructions were also included in the books.

One area of importance noted by students within the content and resources category was the terminology used by the course designers. Confusion of terms was considered by the researchers as a hindrance stress. There was confusion over the terms assessment, evaluation, peer review, and rubric. Students from different parts of the world had different understandings of these terms. The instructors and students worked together within the discussion forums and synchronous meetings to clarify the terminology and to come to a common understanding of definitions.

Another prominent theme in the data was the challenge stress of learning to effectively use new technology tools incorporated into the course. This challenge stress fell under several framework parameters including learning strategies design, navigation, and visual design. The technology tools discussed in the data were the synchronous meeting breakout activity in Adobe Connect and the discussion forums, database activity, and workshop activity in the Moodle LMS.

The affective (learning) connections category of the framework received the fewest coding instances from the data set. Student statements falling into the affective connections category were mainly marked under the satisfaction parameter.

Positive Feedback

The amount of positive feedback noted by students throughout the 16 weeks emerged in the analysis of data. In particular, the students expressed positive feedback for the synchronous sessions and found value in these meetings for tying the activities together and clarifying expectations. One student explained that these meetings were grounding and helped the student remain accountable and connected with the teacher and peers. It was also noted that the synchronous meetings were excellent for collaborating and allowed students to talk through things in voice rather than text. A small number of comments described the synchronous meetings as a waste of time. Presumably, those without questions benefited less than those in need of clarification. Additionally, students were pleased with the emphasis on pedagogy over technology. Students also appreciated the amount, level of, and promptness of feedback.

DISCUSSION AND CONCLUSIONS

Usability evaluations may benefit from the identification of hindrance and challenge stress (see Figure 1). Usability concerns that result in hindrance stress should be mitigated, while those resulting in challenge stress should be appropriately supported and paced.

Hindrance stress detracts from the learning experience. It prohibits the learner from progressing efficiently. The concept of hindrance stress is well aligned with traditional usability evaluations. Hindrance stressors build barriers to achievement of the goals and objectives of a course (Cavanaugh et al., 2000). These stressors should be identified and reduced whenever possible. The results of this study indicated that hindrance stressors might include working across different time zones, scheduling difficulties among collaborators, students dropping the course, and confusion of terminology. Course designers should be sensitive to students' geographical locations and make accommodations so that students can work without excessive

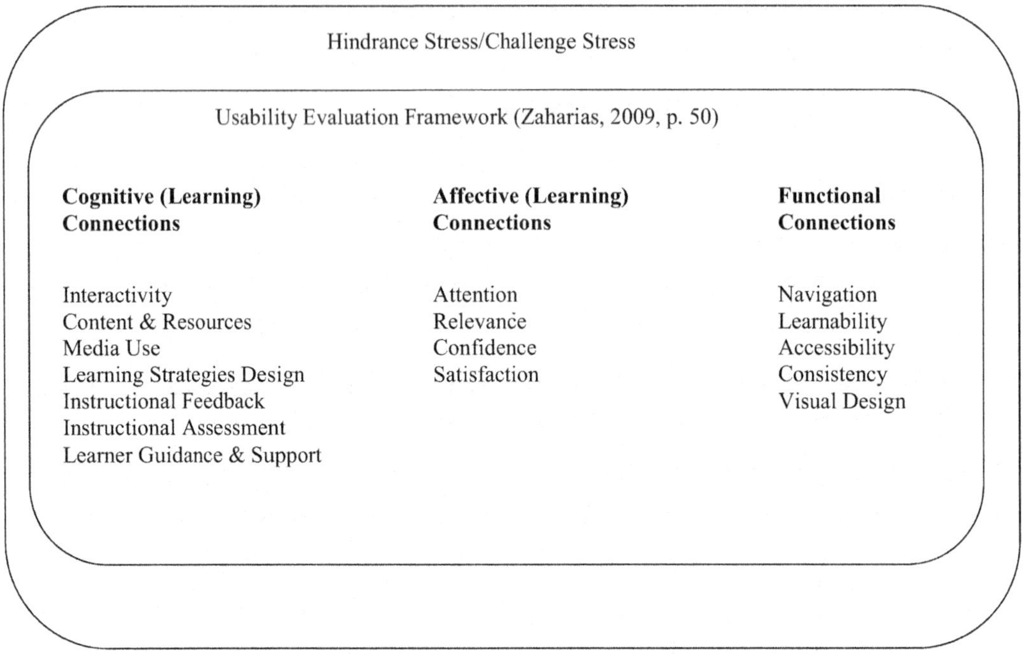

FIGURE 1
Classification Scheme for Analysis of Student Experiences

stress from geographical barriers. Course designers should also be aware of differences in language usage. A course glossary might be included to alleviate conflicting interpretations of terms and to raise awareness of the different uses of terms. Course designers should make a plan for adjusting or reallocating collaborative work in the event that students quit the course prematurely.

Further, course designers should not underestimate the energy and time required to build relationships among classmates to the degree that students can satisfactorily and effectively collaborate. For some students, limiting the number of people in a collaborative group may be beneficial. The findings of this study suggested that some students may benefit from working in an online synchronous meeting setting where voice and video options can enhance the collaboration. Other students may prefer and benefit most from working independently. Likewise, Zaharias and Poulymenakou (2007) noted that "catering for

cultural diversity seems imperative in the design of e-learning courses or technologies for international use" (p. 748). The approach to grouping students is something for course designers and instructors to consider.

At the same time, usability evaluation should examine and evaluate the intensity of challenge stress. Pacing challenges could be thought of as scaffolding: giving learners manageable challenges that increase in difficulty. As the challenges become more difficult, the learners gain more understanding, skills, and the confidence that allows them to tackle larger challenges with a tolerable stress level. The challenge stress experienced by the learner should remain more or less constant as the challenges increase. Carefully paced challenge stressors may balance feelings of frustration with motivation to overcome challenges.

The concept of challenge stress is perhaps better associated with learning theories and pedagogy than traditional usability evaluation. Zaharias (2009), however, argues that the assessment of pedagogy implementation should be incorporated in a usability evaluation framework. The implications of this study indicate that instructors should consider limiting and pacing the challenge stressors they introduce to the class. Students who are new to online learning may experience excessive stress due to the challenge of learning in a new environment. Many tools exist to support social constructivist collaboration; however, students may feel overwhelmed by the technology and learning how to effectively use a large number of different tools. These students may not benefit from a myriad of tools for collaboration (e.g., wikis, databases, discussion forums). Instead, frustration and dissatisfaction may result from such a high learning curve. Adequately training students to use the tools is expected to improve students' success and satisfaction in an online course. Thus, the best teaching tools for the job are only the best if their use does not overly stress students. Reducing the variety of tools along with heavily supporting the collaborative learning activities in a social constructivist course may improve the pacing of challenge stressors. The results of this study suggest limiting and pacing the amount of social interaction and collaboration tools in an online course.

Additionally, the findings of this study suggest that synchronous meetings may be beneficial in supporting students as they are introduced to assignments and as they collaborate. Synchronous meetings allow students to voice their thoughts and concerns and receive immediate feedback. Additionally, instructors and more experienced peers are on hand to help students having technical difficulties. Incorporating synchronous meetings may help instructors manage stress experienced by students.

Affective (learning) connections were not prominent in the data set. Collecting data through general discussion forums and usability-oriented feedback questions, as done in this study, was likely not sufficient for collecting affective experiences. For future research, we suggest incorporating questions about affective experiences into the weekly feedback questions.

Further research toward a framework of usability attributes to evaluate a social constructivist online course may help instructors meet evaluation needs in ways that better support the nature of social constructivist courses. Examining usability through the lens of challenge and hindrance stress sheds light on the type and import of problems and struggles that students experience in an online course. Identifying hindrance stress in order to eliminate barriers to learning fulfills the traditional role of usability evaluation. Optimizing challenge stress in order to manage the pace and intensity of learning experiences may help to bring learning theories and pedagogy into the realm of usability evaluation.

REFERENCES

Blandin, B. (2003). Usability evaluation of online learning programs: A sociological standpoint. In C. Ghaoui (Ed.), *Usability evaluation of online learning programs* (pp. 313–330). Hershey, PA: Information Science.

Brown, S. A., Fuller, R. M., & Vician, C. (2004). Who's afraid of the virtual world? Anxiety and computer-mediated communication. *Journal of the Association for Information Systems*, 5(2), 79–107.

Cavanaugh, M. A., Boswell, W. R., Roehling, M. V., & Boudreau, J. W. (2000). An empirical examination of self-reported work stress among U.S. managers. *Journal of Applied Psychology*, 85(1), 65–74.

Cennamo, K., & Kalk, D. (2005). *Real world instructional design*. Belmont, CA: Wadsworth.

Dumas J. S., & Redish J. C. (1999). *A practical guide to usability testing*. Portland, OR: Intellect.

Edwards, D. J. (1986). *The evaluation of an earth science course at the Open University* (Unpublished doctoral dissertation). Open University, United Kingdom.

Faulkner, L. (2003). Beyond the five-user assumption: Benefits of increased sample sizes in usability testing. *Behavior Research Methods, Instruments, & Computers*, 35(3), 379–383.

Fisher, E. A., & Wright, V. H. (2010). Improving online course design through usability testing. *MERLOT Journal of Online Learning and Teaching, 6*(1), 228–245.

Genov, A. (2009). Usability testing with real data. *Journal of Usability Studies, 4*(2), 85–92.

Grabinger, S., Dunlap, J. C., & Duffield, J. A. (1997). Rich environments for active learning in action: Problem-based learning. *Research in Learning Technology, 5*(2), 5–17.

Joëls, M., Pu, Z., Wiegert, O., Oitzl, M. S., & Krugers, H. J. (2006). Learning under stress: How does it work? *TRENDS in Cognitive Science, 10*(4), 152–158.

Keaton, S. A., & Bodie, G. D. (2011). Explaining social constructivism. *Communication Teacher, 25*(4), 192–196. doi:10.1080/17404622.2011 .601725

Keller, J. M. (1983). Motivational design of instruction. In C. M. Reigeluth (Ed.), *Instructional design theories and models: An overview of their current status* (pp. 383–434). Hillsdale, NJ: Erlbaum.

LePine, J. A., LePine, M. A., & Jackson, C. L. (2004). Challenge and hindrance stress: Relationships with exhaustion, motivation to learn, and learning performance. *Journal of Applied Psychology, 89*(5), 883–891.

Marton, F. (1986). Phenomenography–A research approach to investigating different understandings of reality. *Journal of Thought, 21*(3), 28–49.

Marton, F., & Booth, S. (1997). *Learning and awareness.* Mahwah, NJ: Lawrence Erlbaum.

McCracken, J. R. (2002). *Phenomenographic instructional design: Case studies in geological mapping and materials science* (Unpublished doctoral dissertation). Open University, United Kingdom.

Mendoza, V., & Novick, D. G. (2005). Usability over time. In *Proceedings of the 23rd annual International Conference on Design of Communication: Documenting & Designing for Pervasive Information* (pp. 151–158). New York, NY: ACM.

Mughal, S., Walsh, J., & Wilding, J. (1996). Stress and work performance: The role of trait anxiety. *Personality and Individual Differences, 20*(6), 685–691.

Nielson, J., & Landauer, T. K. (1993). A mathematical model of the finding of usability problems. In *Proceedings of the INTERACT'93 and CHI'93 Conference on Human Factors in Computing Systems* (pp. 206–213). New York, NY: ACM.

Piskurich, G. M. (2006). *Rapid instructional design: Learning ID fast and right.* San Francisco, CA: John Wiley & Sons.

Robinson, H., Phillips, A., Moore, M., & Sheffield, A. (2014). Rich environments for active learning (REALs): A model for online instruction. In S. Keengwe & J. Agamba (Eds.), *Models for improving and optimizing online and blended learning in higher education.* Hersey, PA: IGI.

Rubin, J. (1994). *Handbook of usability testing: How to plan, design, and conduct effective tests.* New York, NY: Wiley.

Sarason, I. G. (1984). Stress, anxiety, and cognitive interference: Reactions to tests. *Journal of Personality and Social Psychology, 46*(4), 929.

Sandbergh, J. (1997). Are phenomenographic results reliable? *Higher Education Research & Development, 16*(2014), 203–212. doi:10.1080/ 0729436970160207

Stress. (1999). In *Merriam-Webster's collegiate dictionary* (10th ed., p. 1164). Springfield, MA: Merriam-Webster.

Tam, M. (2000). Constructivism, instructional design, and technology: Implications for transforming distance learning. *Educational Technology & Society, 3*(2), 50–60.

Virzi, R. A. (1992). Refining the test phase of usability evaluation: How many subjects is enough? *Human Factors, 34*(4), 457–468.

Vygotsky, L. S. (1978). *Mind in society.* Cambridge, MA: Harvard University Press.

Zaharias, P. (2005). E-learning design quality: A holistic conceptual framework. In C. Howard, J. Boettcher, L. Justice, K. Schenk, P. L. Rogers, G. A. Berg, (Eds.), *Encyclopedia of distance learning* (pp. 763–771). New York, NY: Idea Group.

Zaharias, P. (2009). Usability in the context of e-learning: A framework augmenting "traditional" usability constructs with instructional design and motivation to learn. *International Journal of Technology and Human Interaction, 5*(4), 37–59. doi:10.4018/jthi.2009062503

Zaharias, P., & Poylymenakou, A. (2009). Developing a usability evaluation method for e-learning applications: Beyond functional usability. *International Journal of Human-Computer Interaction, 25*(1), 75–98. doi:10.1080/1044731080 2546716

AN ANALYSIS OF TECHNOLOGICAL ISSUES EMANATING FROM FACULTY TRANSITION TO A NEW LEARNING MANAGEMENT SYSTEM

Mapopa William Sanga

Southwestern Oklahoma State University

This case study investigated the process 119 faculty members underwent as they transitioned from using Desire to Learn (D2L) learning management system (LMS), to using Canvas LMS. Other than analyzing technological issues faculty members encountered while navigating various aspects of the Canvas interface, the study also analyzed technological issues faculty members come across while integrating software applications that work in Canvas. These applications included: Panopto, VoiceThread, Respondus Lockdown Browser, and Turnitin. The study presents implications to faculty members, instructional designers, and administrators.

INTRODUCTION

Internet-based learning management systems (LMSs) such as Blackboard, Moodle, WebCT, Canvas, Scholar, and Desire2Learn are some of the popular Internet technologies that support distance, face-to-face, and hybrid/blended teaching-learning processes (Connolly, MacArthur, Stansfield, & McLellan, 2007; Dahlstrom, Brooks, & Bichsel, 2014; DeNeui & Dodge 2006; El Mansour & Mupinga 2007; McGill & Hobbs, 2008). An LMS can be defined as "a self-contained webpage with embedded instructional tools that permit faculty to organize academic content and engage students in their learning" (Gautreau, 2011, p. 2). Again, Alias and Zainuddin (2005) an LMS as "a software application or web-based technology used to plan, implement, and assess a specific learning process" (p. 28). Another definition still, looks at LMSs as web-based technologies that provide instructors with a way to create and deliver content, to monitor student participation and engagement, and to assess student performance online (Venter, van Rensburg, & Davis, 2012). What is common in all these definitions is that an LMS is a web-based application that supports teaching and learning by enabling instructors to create and organize content for learners.

• **Mapopa William Sanga**, assistant professor and teaching and learning coordinator, Southwestern Oklahoma State University. Telephone: (580) 774-7128. E-mail: mapopa.sanga@swosu.edu

The Quarterly Review of Distance Education, Volume 17(1), 2016, pp. 11–21
ISSN 1528-3518
Copyright © 2016 Information Age Publishing, Inc.

LMSs are a technology that enables the communication of course expectations through various resources such as a syllabus, as well as of assignment instructions, grades, and instructional materials (Rubin, Fernandes, Avgerinou, & Moore, 2010). As Bonk and Reynolds (1997) observed, the paradigm shift from traditional educational environments to online educational environments in higher education can also be seen as a challenge to create an active and interactive learning environment, one that gives the learner opportunity to engage and think in multiple ways. In a study that investigated technology adoption into teaching and learning by university faculty, for example, Nicolle (2005) found the link between effective teaching and the use of technology to be critical in helping faculty through the process of integration. As Baia (2009) observed, university faculty members are concerned with effective teaching; hence, if they perceive technology as having a positive impact toward this effort, they are likely to get motivated to integrate it in their teaching.

Several scholars have investigated how faculty and students value and use an LMS in teaching and learning. Pajo and Wallace (2001) stressed that successful integration of technology in teaching depends not only on availability of technology but also on how instructors embrace and use it. In a survey on faculty attitudes on technology, most faculty reported using an LMS, but using limited features as follows: posting course syllabus (78%), recording grades (58%), and communicating with students (52%). Only 20% of faculty reported using the LMS to record lecture content (Jaschik & Lederman, 2014). Recent LMS studies suggest that a variety of system issues, such as suitability of design in screen and system, easiness of course procedure, interoperability of system, easiness of instruction management and appropriateness of multimedia use, flexibility of interaction and test, learner control, variety of communication and test types and user accessibility are important LMS features that directly or indirectly benefit LMSs or e-learning users and influence their attitudes toward LMSs (Fathema & Sutton, 2013; Kim & Leet, 2008; Panda & Mishra, 2007; Pituch & Lee, 2006; Russell, Bebell, O'Dwyer, & O'Connor, 2003; Weaver, Spratt, & Nair, 2008). The literature further indicates that other studies on LMS have focused on how faculty and students value and use an LMS in teaching and learning. Yet more studies have focused on faculty perceptions on the whole transition process to a new LMS. Against this background, it was found necessary to also identify specific technological issues faculty members encounter while transitioning to a new LMS and how such issues can best be mitigated.

PURPOSE OF STUDY

LMSs enable the communication of course expectations through various resources such as a syllabus, as well as of assignment instructions, grades, and instructional materials (Rubin et al., 2010). The present study investigated the process 119 faculty members at a state university in the southern part of the United States went through as they transitioned from using Desire to Learn (D2L) learning management system to using Canvas. The study did not only analyze issues faculty encountered while navigating aspects of the Canvas interface per se, but also issues they came across while integrating other technological applications that work in Canvas. So, apart from general Canvas interface challenges, intricate issues emanated from using four applications leading to the subsequent revision of workshops for the future. The study presents implications to instructional designers, administrators and faculty members on the intricate process of implementing new educational technologies and the best way to manage learning management system transition all together. Specifically, the study sought to answer the following questions:

- What general Canvas interface issues did faculty members face in transition from D2L?
- What issues did faculty members encounter while integrating various software applications in Canvas?
- What implications did these issues have on preparing future faculty development workshops?

RESEARCH DESIGN AND METHODOLOGY

Context and Participants

A state university in the southern part of United States had been using Desire to Learn LMS in the past. An administrative decision led to a switch. While the University administration made the decision to switch, campuswide consultations with faculty members were made for the selection of a new LMS from a shortlist. Canvas was, in the process, selected to be the new LMS the university would be adopting. The Center for Excellence in Teaching and Learning was charged with the task of training faculty members to using Canvas. Between August 2013 and January 2014, 119 faculty members attended four different workshops that primarily focused on training them on how to use and navigate various course-related components in Canvas. Four workshops covering different aspects of Canvas LMS were designed and taught repetitively for a week in October 2013. Workshops were taught again in January 2014, again, repetitively for a week. The majority of the faculty members who took training were those who taught online. However, some faculty members who never taught online also attended the workshops. And so from a total of 119 faculty members, about 95% of these taught online and only about 5% did not.

The four workshops were divided based on sections in the Canvas interface. Again, inevitably, faculty members had to integrate other software applications that work in an LMS. Due to limited time allocated to running the workshops, these applications were not covered deeply in the four workshops since priority was placed on training faculty members on using features of the new LMS rather than add-ons. To that end, it would be found that mastering the latter would pose more challenges to faculty members than general learning of the Canvas interface. A faculty member who is also the teaching and learning coordinator prepared the workshops and ran them repeatedly in collaboration with the director of excellence in teaching and learning. As expected, after scheduled workshops were done, faculty members encountered contextual issues while using Canvas. They would call the teaching and learning coordinator for assistance with various issues while those who needed more specialized assistance would make one-on-one appointments. This was found to be a helpful strategy since it was naturally found that there were varying degrees of technology proficiency among users.

Data Collection

Data for this qualitative study were collected by compiling case study reports on a day-to-day basis. A case study is an empirical inquiry that investigates a contemporary phenomenon in depth and within its real-life context, especially when the boundaries between phenomenon and context are not clearly evident. It is also concerned with studying the phenomenon in context, so that the findings generate insight into how the phenomenon actually occurs within a given situation (Creswell, 2009; Yin, 2009). A Google document (Google doc) was created and all issues faculty raised during workshops, on the telephone, and in one-on-one meetings were systematically recorded on it. After formal workshops, faculty members continued to make calls and hold one-on-one meetings with the teaching and learning coordinator. During these calls and one-on-one meetings, faculty members would raise different issues with Canvas that were addressed by the teaching and learning coordinator. These issues were all recorded on the

Google doc. The recorded notes focused on technological issues users encountered while learning how to navigate the general Canvas interface. The issues ranged from general Canvas interface queries to more complex issues having to do with integrating four software applications: Panopto, Voice Thread, Respondus Lockdown Browser, and Turnitin. While some of these applications, such as Respondus Lockdown Browser. had been used by faculty members in D2L LMS, they still posed a variety of integration issues in Canvas. Notes relating to issues faculty members encountered while navigating the general Canvas interface and while integrating the four external applications were later complied into a detailed case study report from which this study was developed.

Researcher Stance

The teaching and learning coordinator, a faculty member who performs instructional design duties, was the researcher in this study. The researcher, therefore, had the insider's perspective. His initial role began with synthesizing content to be used to facilitate the workshops. He went on to facilitate the workshops by collaborating with the director of Center of Teaching and Learning. All content questions during workshops were addressed by the researcher (the teaching and learning coordinator). The researcher further recorded all the issues raised during workshops on the Google doc that was created for data collection purposes. After formal workshops, users either made calls to the teaching and learning coordinator (the researcher) or made one-on-one appointments. Issues that users inquired about during these calls and meetings were recorded on the Google doc by the researcher. The researcher analyzed the data from which the present artifact was created.

Data Analysis

Data collected from arising issues were analyzed based on two categories. Category

One was comprised of general Canvas interface issues, while Category Two was comprised of issues deriving from integration of four the software applications. While there was an enormous amount of data collected over a period of Canvas delving, whole text analysis was used to examine the notes recorded on the Google doc. This technique requires the researcher to fully understand the purpose of the study to enable continuous study of the data in order to identify specific codes. This procedure for analysis was developed by Glaser and Strauss (1967) and Strauss and Corbin (1998). From the theme "technological issues arising from faculty use of a new learning management system," the two categories are presented in Tables 1 and 2.

FINDINGS

Research Question 1: What general Canvas interface issues did faculty members face in transition from D2L?

Data mostly collected from faculty calls and one-on-one meetings with the teaching and learning coordinator (refer to Table 1) indicated that, as faculty members went to apply the skills they had learned in the workshops, contextual issues arose as they navigated various aspects of the Canvas interface. An instructional design role is about problem solving, it can be argued. Some of the Canvas issues faculty members encountered were resolved within minutes simply by showing an instructor how it is done. These were categorized as Level One issues. Other issues, however, took a reasonable amount of effort to be resolved. These were categorized as Level Two issues and were mostly resolved face to face with a faculty member. Yet other issues took a substantial amount of research, including involving contacting Canvas and other relevant software providers on behalf of faculty members or with them. The latter were categorized as Level Three issues. Level One issues like how to change course dates or deciphering meaning of the various quiz icons were

TABLE 1

General Canvas Interface Issues Encountered by Faculty Members

- How to edit and change course dates?
- What do I do to give true extra credit in Canvas?
- How to enter paper submission grades into grade book.
- How do I enable students attach files to discussion posts?
- What do the various quiz icons stand for?
- How do I import question banks from an external source.
- Moderating a quiz to give more time to students.
- Is it possible to reinstate an exam I deleted accidentally?
- Is it possible to reinstate grades for a student who was removed from my course?
- How is a new column created in the grade book?
- How do I weight my final grade based on various graded events?
- Holding quiz results from student view.
- How do I generate an attendance report in Canvas?
- How do I save and print speed grader comments along with the submitted paper?
- How is a new set of student groups in Canvas created?
- Viewing course analytics without going to the "people" page.
- How is an external calendar feed added to a Canvas account?
- How do I use fudge points in speed grader?
- How do I give a letter grade?
- I cannot see course modules in student view even though I have enabled them for students.
- My announcements are not going out but I feel like I have done everything correctly.
- I have old assignments from two years past still appearing under syllabus and was confusing students. How do I get rid of them?
- Is it possible to be gradually giving feedback to the same assignment throughout a semester?

TABLE 2

Issues Arising From Integrating External Applications Into Canvas

Voice Thread
- Students are not able to see one another's Voice Thread projects, yet all settings were done correctly.
- Students able to create their own voice threads, they can see the instructor's, but cannot comment on one another's.
- Voice Thread project not available on campus computers, yet students are able to view them from outside.
- In going to student view, when I click on the Voice Thread project in one of my modules, I have to sign in. Normally, I am not supposed to do that.
- Unlike with audio comments, I cannot upload my video comment to class Voice Thread project.

Panopto
- Recorded a project in Panopto but do not know where to go in order to save it.
- Students cannot create Panopto projects to make recordings of their work.
- Panopto asks students to sign-in while in the course.
- Cannot see my Panopto video when in Internet Explorer.
- How best do I use Panopto recordings to run a flipped classroom?

Turnitin and Grademark
- When I use Grademark to give feedback, students cannot see comments I make.
- How do I enable students print out Grademark grades and my feedback?
- How do I have Turnitin process an assignment that was submitted before I enabled the app in my course?
- I can see my Grademark comments but students cannot.
- Submissions not generating an originality score with Turnitin due to a "class does not exist" error.

(Table continues on next page)

TABLE 2

(Continued)

Respondus Lockdown Browser
- How to align quiz content between Respondus and Canvas.
- I have disabled the Lockdown browser link in my course so students do not have access to it but even myself cannot locate it.
- Students can't get exams in Respondus to open fully.
- How do I print Canvas tests using Respondus?
- Receiving error message "unable to connect to the test bank network server"
- Several students email me stating that Respondus wouldn't work. Something about saying it had no Internet connection but they could get to the Internet just fine if they were not using that. Was there a server issue?
- I have had multiple students stating that Respondus didn't prompt them to use the webcam. Settings for Respondus Monitor look correct. Why is it allowing them to take the quiz without the webcam?

TABLE 3

General Observations

- General Canvas interface questions came up during workshops, more contextual, specific issues arose while using Canvas after workshops.
- Six months after scheduled workshops, basic issues to do with importing content from the expiring D2L still came up.
- Most serious issues arose from faculty use of external applications in Canvas.
- Most users who had reservations about Canvas at the beginning, ended up liking it later when they started using it.
- There was variation in speed of mastery of the new LMS among users.
- In due course, more faculty members who did not teach online ended up wanting to learn Canvas.
- Faculty members who did not teach online found features like the gradebook very helpful in managing student grades.
- Issues faculty members encountered helped the designer to go back and formatively evaluate and revise workshops.

resolved with a simple explanation or demonstration. Level Two issues like how to give true extra credit or how to import question banks form an external source or indeed how to moderate a quiz in order to allocate more time to specific students required a well prepared tutorial to faculty members. Depending on how quickly a faculty member would master the action, steps would be repeated mostly in a one-on-one meeting until the user was able to perform the required action on his or her own. Even more interesting were Level Three issues such as importing quiz banks from an external source, reinstating a deleted quiz, reinstating grades for a student who had been dropped from a course, and others. While the first task, importing quiz banks from an external source, would be done with the faculty member, the other two issues, reinstating grades and deleted quizzes, could not be handled at the level of Canvas access of a college administrator. These would therefore require

the teaching and learning Coordinator contacting Canvas by either creating a ticket or using the chat feature. Later on, faculty members were walked through creating tickets of their own and being able to use the chat feature to have such type of Level Three issues resolved. This strategy allied well the philosophy of doing it together in instructional design (Dick, Carey, & Carey, 2009).

Research Question 2: What issues did faculty members encounter while integrating various software applications in Canvas?

All issues that arose from integrating the four external applications into Canvas were categorized as Level Three issues due to the depth of their complexity. From a general perspective, the integration of these applications posed more challenging issues to faculty members than general Canvas interface use.

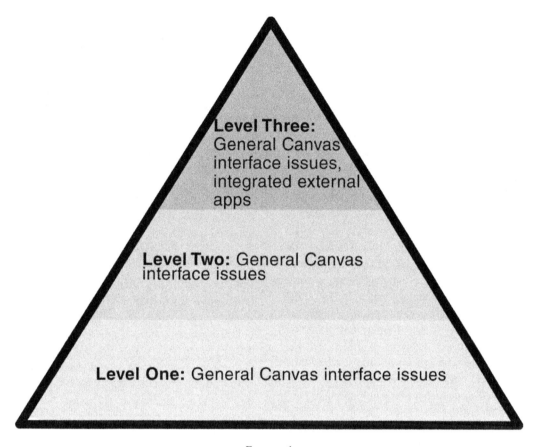

FIGURE 1
The Three Levels

Voice Thread

A Voice Thread is a dynamic, living conversation space that can be altered anytime. Basically, the application is about creating collaborative space with video, voice and text commenting (Voice Thread, 2015).

Issues with Voice Thread, such as students not being able to see one another's projects when the instructor felt they had done all the settings correctly, posed an intricate challenge to solve. The same applied to issues like a Voice Thread project not available on on-campus computers. These issues required very systemic diagnosis, which began by asking the instructor for very specific details of what exactly was happening. The diagnosis would take place through e-mail or telephone. Once details of the problem were made clear, the teaching and learning coordinator would identify solutions that would essentially solve the problem. Again, the whole process would be done while doing it together with the faculty member rather than doing it on their behalf. Interestingly, though, some faculty members would ask that the problem be solved for them rather than work through it together. This simply highlighted varying faculty preferences when it comes to solving technological issues. Procedurally, issues that could not be solved at the level of access of on-campus Voice Thread administrators would require creating a ticket with Voice Thread engineers who would in turn examine the problem and offer solutions.

Panopto

Panopto is a software package for businesses and universities that makes it easy for anyone to record, live stream, and share video (Panopto, 2015). In education institutions, Panopto is mostly used for lecture capture. Faculty members would normally record a lecture with video and/or PowerPoint and in turn post it in a module for students to view at any time. For example, an instructor wanted to find out how best to use Panopto to run a face-to-face flipped classroom. This scenario actually justified the application's valuable use. While working with the instructor, the Teaching and Learning Coordinator suggested that the best way to do it would be to make Panopto recordings of all lessons and post them in a module, for example, and set each lesson recording to open a few days prior to when they would be taught. That way, students would watch the stream prior and in turn discuss it when they came to class. Another interesting issue involved students not being able to make Panopto recordings themselves as the instructor had asked them to. While running a diagnosis of this issue, it was found that the instructor had actually made the settings in such a way that only teachers could create projects. This made sense in the context, considering that the University had purchased licensing for the application primarily for lecture capture and for student view. Finally, some issues that faculty members encountered with Panopto made the Teaching and Learning Coordinator offer the advice that sometimes it was a browser issue as the application did not normally work well in Internet Explorer. To that end, Google Chrome and Firefox were made recommended browsers.

Turnitin and Grademark

Turnitin is an Internet-based plagiarism-prevention service that enables submitted essays to be checked for unoriginal content. It normally integrates with Grademark, which enables instructors to grade students' written work online by providing them the ability to add comments within the body of a paper, point out grammar and punctuation mistakes or works of art (Turnitin, 2015).

One of the pertinent issues that faculty members encountered while using Turnitin and Grademark was a scenario where they would give feedback through commenting and pointing but students could not see the comments. As seemingly complicated as it looked, sometimes the issue had to do with the browser students were using as Turnitin, we learned, works best in Firefox and Google Chrome. Yet interestingly, in certain instances, it still posed varying issues with the two browsers. Apart from browser issues, sometimes the application would just malfunction without any reasonable diagnosable cause. These latter issues would occur from time to time in some sort of a flare. When such was the case, the teaching and learning coordinator would create a ticket with Turnitin engineers who would then look into the issues and mostly elucidated them by pointing out the complexity of having to integrate an LMS and two external applications that have to complement one another. In certain instances, faculty members would have issues with Turnitin failing to process essays that were submitted before the application was enabled in a particular assignment. In such a scenario, instructors would be advised to have students resubmit the assignments after it (the application) had been turned on. Also, sometimes server issues would bring a glitch, which resulted in submissions not generating an originality score due to a "class does not exist" error. Being server issues, Turnitin engineers would be asked to look into the problem and do necessary maintenance work. Other issues faculty encountered would, for example, be students' inability to print out feedback provided through Grademark. To address an issue like this one, the teaching and learning coordinator would devise a series of steps and walk the concerned faculty member through them so they would offer proper assistance to students.

Respondus Lockdown Browser

Respondus is a tool for creating and managing exams that can be printed to paper or published directly to an LMS. It is a custom browser that locks down the testing environment within an LMS such as Canvas. When students use Respondus LockDown Browser, they are unable to print, copy, go to another URL, or access other applications. When an assessment is started, students are locked into it until they submit it for grading. It is complemented by Respondus Monitor, a companion application that integrates webcam technology with LockDown Browser (Respondus, 2015).

One of the outstanding issues that faculty would seek assistance for was how to print Canvas tests using Respondus. This would require the teaching and learning coordinator to walk them through steps for performing the action. In certain instances, users would receive an error message while trying to connect to a test bank server after Respondus had been enabled. Such an issue would require figuring out whether it was a Respondus issue or an issue to do with the owner of the test bank they were drawing questions from. Sometimes students would simply report to their instructor that Respondus would not work. Such a very general issue required systematic diagnosis by advising the instructor to ask for more details on what was exactly happening when students attempted to take a test. From that information provided by students, a determination would be made, mostly engaging Respondus engineers to locate the root of the problem, which would be as complex as a server malfunction case. Yet other times, while an instructor had made all the settings correctly enabling Respondus Monitor, students would take a test without being prompted to use a webcam. Again, Respondus engineers would be engaged to look into such a complex glitch.

Research Question 3: What implications did these issues have on preparing future faculty development workshops?

From a general perspective, it was noted that while faculty members mostly asked general Canvas interface questions during workshops, more complex, context-specific issues arose when they went to use Canvas on a daily basis. Also, it was interesting to note that most faculty members who had reservations about Canvas at the beginning of the whole process, preferring to continue with D2L that they had used for a long time, ended up liking it (Canvas) later after learning how to use it. Again, with time, more and more faculty who did not teach online ended up wanting to learn Canvas. This group of faculty members found features like the gradebook and announcements very helpful in managing classes and student work. Overall, the most challenging issues arose from faculty integration of the four applications in Canvas. Naturally, there was variation in speed of mastery of features in the new LMS among faculty members. For example, some users were still learning the basics on a one-on-one basis 6 months after the initial workshops were run. Others, however, only took as less as a couple of weeks after the workshops to get familiar with the whole interface. The variation in speed of mastery, it was learned, was due to different levels of proficiency with technology and also personal enthusiasm and motivation.

In the long run, issues faculty members encountered helped us to go back and formatively evaluate and revise the workshops. Again, the whole philosophy of doing it together in instructional design (Dick et al., 2009) became reminiscent in this study as it was clearly shown that those faculty members who preferred to learn by doing it together with the teaching and learning coordinator easily overcame issues they were encountering with the technology than those who preferred for the teaching and learning coordinator to solve problems for them. Findings of this study indicate that the whole process of implementing faculty development workshops require proper planning between administrators and instructional designers in order to ensure proper allocation of time and other resources, thereby facilitating a more efficient transition from one LMS to another.

IMPLICATIONS

The study presents several implications to instructional designers, faculty members, administrators, and educational software developers on the intricate process of implementing new educational technologies and the best way to manage learning management system transition as a whole. First, while time is always a constraint, it is important to include all aspects of an LMS in a workshop in order to mitigate arising issues when faculty members get down to use it. It is likely that if more workshop time had been allocated to covering integration of the four applications to a deeper level during planning, some of the issues that arose while faculty members used them would have been mitigated. Also, the study does show that faculty members tend to master technological skills faster and more efficiently when they get involved in solving issues with instructional designers rather than having the latter do it for them. Again, while educational software developers do produce applications that integrate well in an LMS such as Canvas, the study showed that there are issues that do arise when the applications are actually used in context. Server issues and sudden malfunction of applications as evidenced in this study provide useful feedback to the administrators of the four applications discussed in this study.

In the end, the whole process of transitioning to a new LMS became an innovation being adopted. To be called an innovation, an idea does not have to be necessarily newly invented (Rogers, 1995; Van de Ven, 1986). As Rogers (2003) contended, one of the distinct innovation attributes is complexity, the extent to which an innovation is considered difficult to learn and utilize. Issues that arose while fac-

ulty members used the new LMS prompted designers to go back and revise workshops in order to make future adoption processes of this type less difficult for users. Finally, the fact that this was a case study of one institution of higher learning is a limitation to this study. Similar studies in other institutions undergoing LMS transition including integrated applications would extend the scope of this study and probably corroborate the present findings.

REFERENCES

Alias, N. A., & Zainuddin, A. M. (2005). Innovation for better teaching and learning: Adopting the learning management system. *Malaysian Online Journal of Instructional Technology, 2*(2), 27–40.

Baia, P. L. (2009). *The role of commitment to pedagogical quality: The adoption of instructional technology in higher education.* Retrieved from http://files.eric.ed.gov/fulltext/ED504055.pdf

Bonk, C. J., & Reynolds, T. H. (1997). Learner-centered Web instruction for higher-order thinking, teamwork, and apprenticeship. In B. H. Khan (Ed.), *Web-based instruction* (pp. 167–178). Englewood Cliffs, NJ: Educational Technology Publications.

Connolly, T. M., MacArthur, E., Stansfield, M., & McLellan, E. (2007). A quasi-experimental study of three online learning courses in computing. *Computers & Education 49*(2), 345–359.

Creswell, J. W. (2009). *Research design: Qualitative, quantitative, and mixed methods approaches* (3rd ed.). London, England: SAGE.

Dahlstrom, E., Brooks, D. C., & Bichsel, J. (2014). The current ecosystem of learning management systems in education: Student, faculty, and IT perspectives (Research report). Louisville, CO: ECAR. Retrieved from http://www.educause.edu/ecar

DeNeui, D. L., & Dodge, T. L. (2006). Asynchronous learning networks and student outcomes: The utility of online learning components in hybrid courses. *Journal of Instructional Psychology, 33*(4), 256–259.

Dick, W., Carey, L., & Carey, J. (2009). *The systematic design of instruction* (7th ed.). Boston, MA: Pearson.

El Mansour, B., & Mupinga, D. M. (2007). Students' positive and negative experiences in hybrid and online classes. *College Student Journal, 41*(1), 242–248.

Fathema, N., & Sutton, K. (2013). Factors influencing faculty members' learning management systems adoption behavior: An analysis using the technology acceptance model. *International Journal of Trends in Economics Management & Technology*, 2(6), 20–28.

Glaser, B. G., & Strauss, A. L. (1967). *The discovery of grounded theory: Strategies for qualitative research.* Chicago, IL: Aldine.

Gautreau, C. (2011). Motivational factors affecting the integration of a learning management system by faculty. *The Journal of Educators Online, 8*(1), 1–25.

Jaschik, S., & Lederman, D. (2014). The 2014 Inside Higher Ed Survey of Faculty Attitudes on Technology: A study by Gallup and Inside HigherEd. *Inside Higher Ed.* Retrieved from https://www.insidehighered.com/news/survey/survey-faculty-attitudes-technology

Kim, S. W., & Leet, M. G. (2008). Validation of an Evaluation model for LMSs. *Journal of Computer Assisted Learning, 24*(4), 284–294. doi:10.1111/j.1365-2729.2007.00260

McGill, T. J., & Hobbs, V. J. (2008). How students and instructors using a virtual learning environment perceive the fit between technology and task. *Journal of Computer Assisted Learning, 24*(3), 191–202. doi:10.1111/j.1365-2729.2007.00253.x

Nicolle, P. M. (2005). *Technology adoption into teaching and learning by mainstream university faculty: A mixed methodology study revealing the "how, when, why and why not"* (Unpublished doctoral dissertation). Louisiana State University and Agricultural and Mechanical College. Baton Rouge, LA.

Pajo, K., & Wallace, C. (2001). Barriers to the uptake of web-based technology by university teachers. *The Journal of Distance Education, 16*(1), 70–84.

Panda, S., & Mishra, S. (2007). E-learning in a mega open university: Faculty attitude, barriers and motivators. *Educational Media International, 44*(4), 323–338. doi:10.1080/09523980701680854

Panopto. (2015). *Why choose Panopto?* Retrieved from http://panopto.com/why-choose-panopto/

Pituch, K. A, & Lee, Y. -K. (2006). The influence of system characteristics on e-learning use. *Computers Education, 47,* 222–244.

Respondus. (2015). *Respondus lockdown browser.* Retrieved from http://www.respondus.com/products/lockdown-browser/index.shtml

Rogers, E. M. (1995). *Diffusion of innovations* (4th ed.). New York, NY: The Free Press.

Rogers, E. M. (2003). *Diffusion of innovations* (5th ed.). New York, NY: Free Press.

Rubin, B., Fernandes, R., Avgerinou, M. D., & Moore, J. (2010). The effect of learning management systems on student and faculty outcomes. *The Internet and Higher Education, 13*(1), 82–83. doi:10.1016/j.iheduc.2009.10.008

Russell, M., Bebell, D., O'Dwyer, L., & O'Connor, K. (2003). Examining teacher technology use: Implications for preservice and inservice teacher preparation. *Journal of Teacher Education, 54*(5), 297–310.

Strauss, A., & Corbin, J. (1998). *Basics of qualitative research techniques and procedures for developing grounded theory* (2nd ed.). London, England: SAGE.

Turnitin. (2015). *Turnitin for higher education.* Retrieved from http://www.turnitin.com/en_us/turnitin-for-higher-education

Van de Ven, A. H. (1986). Central problems in the management of innovation. *Management Science, 32*(5), 590–607.

Venter, P., Van Rensburg, M. J., & Davis, A. (2012). Drivers of learning management system use in a South African open and distance learning institution. *Australasian Journal of Educational Technology, 28*(2), 183–198. Retrieved from http://www.ascilite.org.au/ajet/ajet28/venter.html

Voicethread. (2015). *Text can't replace you: Voice Thread for higher ed.* Retrieved from http://voicethread.com/products/highered/

Weaver, D., Spratt, C., & Nair, C. (2008). Academic and student use of a LMS: Implications for quality. *Australasian Journal of Educational Technology, 24*(1), 30–41.

Yin, R. (2009). *Case Study Research: Design and Methods* (4th ed.). Thousand Oaks, CA: SAGE.

SYNCHRONOUS AND ASYNCHRONOUS COMMUNICATION IN DISTANCE LEARNING
A Review of the Literature

Lynette Watts
Midwestern State University

Distance learning is commonplace in higher education, with increasing numbers of students enjoying the flexibility e-learning provides. Keeping students connected with peers and instructors has been a challenge with e-learning, but as technology has advanced, the methods by which educators keep students engaged, synchronously and asynchronously, also have improved. This literature review presents support for both types of interaction; however, findings indicate educators must consider time constraints, technological ability, and motivation for students to interact in the online setting. Recommendations for implementing both synchronous and asynchronous interactions are made, including technological considerations. Finally, suggestions for research in distance learning are presented for consideration.

INTRODUCTION

Distance learning is no longer the exception in higher education. Students now take their classes with them on their iPads, mobile phones, and other electronic devices. Instead of being required to sit in a classroom for hours at a time, many students take distance courses because of work and social schedules and prefer the flexibility of engaging in their educational experiences in settings of their preference. A major concern of distance learning is the lack of face-to-face student-student interaction and student-instructor interaction,

which has led researchers to seek effective ways to keep students engaged in the distance learning environment (Jones, Morales, & Knezek, 2005; Stein, Wanstreet, Calvin, Overtoom, & Wheaton, 2005). Factors related to engagement are students' connections to their peers and instructors, student motivation, and course outcomes, such as grades (Griffiths & Graham, 2010; Rockinson-Szapkiw & Wendt, 2015; Strang, 2013).

Asynchronous interaction has been the traditional method for engaging students in their distance education courses, but as technology has evolved, synchronous media have become

• **Lynette Watts**, Assistant Professor, Midwestern State University, 3410 Taft Blvd., Bridwell Hall, Ofc 201E, Wichita Falls, TX 76308. Telephone: (940) 397-4833. E-mail: lynette.watts@mwsu.edu

The Quarterly Review of Distance Education, Volume 17(1), 2016, pp. 23–32   ISSN 1528-3518 an increasing focus for engagement in online courses. This literature review was created to present the argument for both types of interaction, including the role both asynchronous and synchronous interactions play in how connected students feel in the online environment; how interactions affect learning, grades, and satisfaction in the online environment; and if student motivation drives the type of interaction in the online environment. Recommendations for implementing both types of interactions are made, including technological considerations. Finally, suggestions for future research in distance learning are presented for consideration.

METHODOLOGY

Articles for this literature review were retrieved from Midwestern State University's Moffett Library Databases: Academic Search Complete, Article First, CINAHL Complete, EdITLib, Education Source, ERIC, PsycARTICLES, Psychology and Behavioral Science Collection, and PsycINFO. Articles were also retrieved from the search engine Google Scholar and by searching the reference lists of relevant articles. Articles selected were peer reviewed and not limited to a date range, though the range of selected articles was between 5 and 11 years from the time this review was written. Key word searches were *distance education and dialogue, asynchronous interactions, synchronous interactions, asynchronous and synchronous interactions in online education, interactions and transactional distance,* and *motivation in asynchronous and synchronous interactions in higher education.* Approximately 70 articles were reviewed, with 24 being chosen because they related to the overall topic of the review and/or provided considerations for future research.

DISCUSSION

Historically, asynchronous interaction made up the majority of contact students had with

their peers and instructors in distance education (Hrastinski, 2008). Asynchronous communication is defined as communication occurring through the use of email and discussion boards, with the instructor playing a larger role as facilitator between students (Hrastinski, 2008; Pan & Sullivan, 2005). The primary benefit of asynchronous dialogue is the flexibility it provides for anytime-anywhere e-learning, which is the main convenience of online learning (Buxton, 2014; Hrastinski, 2008; Stein, Wanstreet, & Calvin, 2009). In addition, prerecorded video allowing students to view media on their own time has recently been included as another component of asynchronous interaction (Griffiths & Graham, 2010). To the contrary, synchronous technology is defined as live streaming video and/or audio with instantaneous feedback (Giesbers, Rienties, Tempelaar, & Gijselaers, 2014; McBrien, Jones, & Cheng, 2009). The goal of either type of interaction is to ensure students are engaged with the learning process so they perceive they are part of the learning process and, as a result, retain the material and feel engaged in the distance learning environment. Table 1 presents a summary of the major studies presented in this review.

Transactional Distance

Moore's (1973) theory of transactional distance is based on the premise students experience a psychological and communications gap in the online environment. Moore posited students must interact with their peers, instructors, and the content to decrease that distance. Moore (1989) described when students interact with the content, they are having an internal dialogue where they think, discuss, and examine the content with themselves. He also noted the interaction students have with instructors is important because students gain the experience from the instructor who is the content expert. Finally, student-to-student interaction is vital because, as students interact with each other, they not only better learn the content, they learn how to navigate group dynamics.

TABLE 1
Summary of the Literature

Citation	Population/Sample Size/Sampling Procedure	Main Findings	Limitations
Buxton, 2014	Pharmacy students/$n = 82$ (41 asynchronous webinar; 41 synchronous webinar)/convenience	Positive responses regarding both forms of interaction; more positive results overall with asynchronous platform	Small data set; lag time between completion of course and survey responses; difference in lecturer style
Chundar & Prakash, 2009	Introductory computer technology course – undergraduate freshmen/$n = 22$/convenience	Time constraints and content need to be considered before implementing synchronous elements; asynchronous interaction was sufficient for learning outcomes	None stated
Duncan, Kenworthy, & McNamara, 2012	Executive MBA students/$n = 272$/convenience	Both types of engagement positively impact overall course grades; asynchronous more positively impacts final exam grades; synchronous more positively impacts overall grades	Assumption that weaker academic students may ask more questions (quantity) but have overall lower grades because quality of interaction is weaker was not tested for
Giesbers, Rienties, Tempelaar, & Gijselaers, 2013	Baccalaureate-level economics course, elective/$n = 110$/convenience	Participants who participated in synchronous conferences participated more in asynchronous interactions; no difference between control- and autonomy-motivated participants' number of asynchronous posts; control-motivated students appeared to be stronger in asynchronous participation, which drove their synchronous participation	This course was an elective, and students chose their levels of participation; students withdrew from this course, which may have indicated no amount of synchronous participation kept them engaged in the course
Griffiths & Graham, 2010	Instructional Psychology & Technology with undergraduates/$n = 150$ (students), $n = 3$ instructors/convenience	Positive reaction from students and instructors using asynchronous interaction (pre-recorded videos); positive feedback that students were engaged in the course and built personal relationships	None stated
Hrastinski, 2008	Two online classes of undergraduates/$n = 27$/convenience	Asynchronous interaction is best for allowing students to reflect on complex information before responding in the discussion board and when students have time constraints not allowing them to be involved in the synchronous forums; synchronous interaction provides motivation to respond and allows for group work, including planning and exchanging of ideas	None stated

(Table continues on next page)

TABLE 1
Summary of the Literature

Citation	Population/Sample Size/Sampling Procedure	Main Findings	Limitations
Mabrito, 2006	Junior and Senior level college business students/n = 16/convenience	Higher quantity of conversations, but they were not as focused on content; asynchronous interactions were more focused on content but generated less conversation; asynchronous interaction included follow-up questions about content; students felt they were more productive in the synchronous interactions but also felt the asynchronous interactions were more effective in completing the writing assignment	None stated
McBrien, Jones, & Cheng, 2009	Undergraduate and graduate level students in various education courses/n = 90/opportunistic	Students felt more connected (less transactional distance) to online courses through synchronous interaction; technological issues caused some dissatisfaction with the experience and increased transactional distance; clear expectations need to be outlined in distance education	Limited sample size and the use of one online synchronous system
Pan, 2008	Graduate students/n = 28/convenience	Familiarize students with synchronous program before beginning the class; synchronous interaction provides high-tech, high-touch experience with just-in-time feedback	None stated
Stein, Wanstreet, & Calvin, 2009	Graduate students in an American literacy course/n = 15/convenience	Providing support for students decreases transactional distance; novice online students should connect with peers to create a time and space for learning; students who exhibit self-motivating behaviors are more likely to engage in the online course	None stated
Rockinson-Szapkiw & Wendt, 2015	Educational technology undergraduate students/n = 109/convenience	The use of multimedia tools results in more effective interaction, generally through synchronous use; asynchronous interaction requires too much cognitive arousal, resulting in less interest in the topic; synchronous interaction may support a sense of community	Limited generalization of results; no qualitative data gathered; limited technologies included in this study
Strang, 2013	Graduate level project management course/n = 38 (control), n = 42 (test)	Synchronous interaction provides more cooperation than asynchronous interaction	Small sample size; findings may not be generalizable to undergraduate population; limited examination of use of email and other collaboration methods

Although Moore (1989) did not address whether the interactions had to be synchronous or asynchronous, his main stipulation was any interaction must support student learning. Several studies have been conducted describing how online interactions influence students' perceptions of transactional distance (Benton, Li, & Brown, 2014; Dammers, 2009; Falloon, 2011; Griffiths & Graham, 2010; Hutti, 2007; Pan & Sullivan, 2005; Schullo, Hibelink, Venable, & Barron, 2007).

Asynchronous Interaction. While it is clear synchronous interaction is playing a larger role in the online learning environment, asynchronous interaction still has its place in distance education. Research indicated asynchronous interactions allow students to take time to consider their thoughts, engage with the content more deeply, feel a part of the learning community, and post more reflective comments in discussion boards (Hrastinski, 2008; Stein et al., 2009). Hrastinski (2008) reported being able to contemplate the content before responding in discussion boards increased cognitive engagement with the content, especially when the content was difficult. However, many respondents did not feel as though they were completely part of the learning community. Stein et al. (2009) also reported participants believed taking the time to reflect on their own ideas as well as their peers' allowed them to interact more deeply with the content.

Buxton (2014) conducted a study of two groups of 41 pharmacy students: one group was enrolled in an asynchronous online course, and the other was enrolled in a synchronous live webinar course. He reported statistically significant findings relating satisfaction of the participants in the asynchronous course to the course meeting their needs (4.8, $p < 0.05$). Although participants were not specifically asked if they missed the live interaction, participants clearly indicated they did learn the material and were very satisfied with the asynchronous nature of the course. The results of these studies indicate the interaction experienced by the learners led to learning and, subsequently, a decrease in transactional dis-

tance and feeling more connected to the course; these findings provide support for Moore's (1973) theory.

Griffiths and Graham (2010) conducted three different case studies among instructors and students in two different online courses using asynchronous video to determine perceptions of immediacy and closeness using this format. The researchers interviewed students during each of the semesters the courses were offered and concluded the asynchronous format of the videos allowed students to feel very connected to the instructors. Students reported satisfaction with the feedback provided and believed the instructor offering the feedback cared about them. Instructors perceived students to engage with the content more deeply when students were able to take time to reflect before recording their video submission. One instructor reported s/he could even perceive the level of students' understanding of the material by examining students' facial cues and voice inflections. These results seem to provide support for Moore's (1973) theory: when students believe they have learned the material, transactional distance decreases.

Synchronous Interaction. Synchronous interaction is becoming a more integral part of communication among students and between students and their instructors. Through the advancement of technology, asynchronous communication is no longer the only method of linking students in an online classroom. Researchers have continued to investigate the use of synchronous technology to determine if these types of interaction are more beneficial than asynchronous interactions in the online learning environment (Giesbers et al., 2014; McBrien et al., 2009; Rockinson-Szapkiw & Wendt, 2015). Research in distance learning has suggested students view synchronous interactions positively because of instantaneous feedback, being able to see their classmates, and because they report feeling more engaged in the online experience (Falloon, 2011; Hrastinski, 2008; Stein et al., 2009; Strang, 2013). No matter what technology is used, one particular issue with synchronous interactions is potential student scheduling conflicts with the live meeting times. These conflicts could lead to frustration with the online environment and, therefore, lead to less satisfaction and feeling disconnected from the learning environment (Chundur & Prakash, 2009; Falloon, 2011; Hrastinski, 2008).

Hrastinski (2008) conducted a study of 27 students to examine differences in perception about asynchronous and synchronous interactions. Participants offered insight that the synchronous interactions felt more like talking, and students engaged more with their peers. In addition to improved social interactions with their peers, students also reported an advantage of synchronous interactions was the ability to monitor classmates' reactions during discussions, which led to psychological arousal (motivation) to continue engaging with their peers.

As has been demonstrated through various research studies, results suggest students appreciate the synchronous interaction of online learning and feel a connection to peers and instructors. Students appreciate receiving instantaneous feedback, are able to observe visual cues from peers, and report they feel a very social connection in their online courses. All of these positive results lead to students feeling a decrease in transactional distance; in other words, they do not necessarily need to be in the physical presence of other students to learn and feel a sense of accomplishment, again providing support for Moore's (1973) theory.

Combining Synchronous and Asynchronous Interaction. Asynchronous and synchronous interactions can be used concurrently, but students have not always reported positive outcomes. McBrien et al. (2009) reported 9% of participants (*n* = 62) became frustrated when trying to listen to the audio, type responses, and view the PowerPoint presentations. The researchers concluded the frustrated students did not feel as connected to the course, and their sense of transactional distance increased. Participants also reported feelings of frustra-

tion when they experienced technical difficulties and recommended instructors in online learning consider offering training with the synchronous platform before the class started. Pan and Sullivan (2005) also suggested providing technical training with an added caution to instructors not to make the assumption all students are proficient, or even familiar, with online learning platforms and other live streaming programs. These findings are important, as students' feelings of becoming overwhelmed and frustrated may lead to an increase in transactional distance in online learning. As discussed, both asynchronous and synchronous interactions keep students engaged in the online setting. When students are engaged, course outcomes, such as learning, grades, and satisfaction, tend to also improve.

Course Outcomes

Course outcomes may be described in terms of perceived learning, grades, and satisfaction with the learning experience. These factors have all been examined in the literature as related to distance learning, and these findings, while not always statistically significant, can provide educators who teach online courses with important information about using each form to enhance course outcomes. Some researchers have specifically examined asynchronous and synchronous interactions in terms of connectedness and how this connectedness translates to final group project grades, final exam grades, and final course grades.

Final Project Grades. Two different studies reported on graduate students' interactions and their relation to final course grades. Strang (2013) studied a total of 81 students in two different groups (*n* = 38 in the control group [asynchronous] and *n* = 42 in the test group [synchronous]). After controlling for such influences as course content, instructor, course requirements, prior ability, identical meeting times, team abilities, and randomized treatment groups, Strang (2013) concluded the synchronous group collaborated more in-depth and achieved a higher final project grade. The result was statistically significant at the 95% confidence level.

Final Exam Grades. Strang's (2013) study strengthened the results presented by Duncan, Kenworthy, and McNamara (2012), who studied 272 graduate students enrolled in an online accounting program to determine if participation in synchronous and asynchronous forums led to higher final exam scores and higher overall course grades. Overall, when quality increased in both synchronous and asynchronous forums, final exam score increased; alternately, Duncan et al. (2012) reported higher numbers of interaction between students led to decreases in the final exam scores because many of the discussions were not related to course content. Analysis of synchronous and asynchronous interactions separately on overall course grade revealed a statistical significance (at the 5% and 10% confidence levels, respectively), with a higher statistical significance with synchronous interaction. Finally, the quality of both synchronous and asynchronous interactions was positively related to final exam and overall course scores but significantly related only to the final course scores ($p < 0.05$; $p = 0.029$).

Final Course Grades. Rockinson-Szapkiw and Wendt (2015) conducted a study of 109 graduate students to determine if either synchronous or asynchronous interaction had an effect on assignment points. Following statistical testing, the researchers concluded synchronous interaction resulted in more collaboration and a higher final grade than asynchronous interaction. Although they reached similar conclusions as Strang (2013), their findings were not statistically significant, as they reported only a small effect size, as defined by Cohen's threshold (small effect size is .01; partial $\eta^2 = 0.04$).

Perceived Satisfaction With Interaction Formats. A few assumptions were presented relating to why synchronous interaction led to higher final course grades. Rockinson-Szapkiw and Wendt (2015) concluded the richness of synchronous technologies enhance the learning environment by decreasing cognitive load and lessening ambiguity. Pan and Sullivan (2005) reported similar positive outcomes with Skype as a learning platform; even though this study was conducted when the concept of Skype was relatively new, students reported this type of interaction enhanced interaction and allowed students to receive immediate feedback, receive reinforcement for important concepts, and develop a working relationship with members of the class through what the authors deemed a high-tech, high touch learning platform.

Although previous studies suggested the richness of synchronous interactions, other studies discussed problems related to synchronous interactions in the online classroom. Chundur and Prakash (2009) conducted a case study of 22 students to compare asynchronous and synchronous forms of interaction, and their findings contradicted previous research. Chundur and Prakash (2009) reported approximately 23% of respondents felt asynchronous interaction such as e-mail and discussion boards were useful and increased their learning outcomes. Only 42% felt the same way about the synchronous meetings because scheduling issues prevented many students from attending the live sessions. These findings were similar to Mabrito (2006), who reported synchronous interactions were more unfocused and did not relate as much to course content while asynchronous interactions typically revealed deeper content discussions. Surprisingly, 16 participants felt their asynchronous discussions were valued more in terms of content participation (75%), students preferred the synchronous interactions (100%), and results suggest students interacted more with each other through those interactions.

Motivation

Much research has been conducted suggesting the importance of considering motivation as a characteristic of successful distance education students, but few recent studies exist related to how motivation for one interacting synchronously may drive the motivation for interacting asynchronously and vice versa. The consideration of motivation may be an area for further exploration because of the plethora of asynchronous and synchronous interacting methods available to students. Hrastinski (2008) analyzed 27 participants' synchronous and asynchronous communications from two different online courses and interviewed 12 participants about their experiences with the two types of communication. He reported psychological effects students experienced during synchronous interactions provide motivation to continuously be engaged with peers, providing a more social aspect to the learning experience.

Giesebers et al. (2014) took the notion of this psychological need to engage one step further to determine if participation in synchronous interaction led to increased engagement in asynchronous interaction. They conducted a study of 110 undergraduates and hypothesized self-motivated students who participated in synchronous discussion with peers would also post more in the asynchronous forums. The researchers determined academic motivation, and students were categorized as either autonomy motivated or control motivated. Autonomy motivated is characterized by intrinsic (pure enjoyment) and extrinsic (the right thing to do) factors while control oriented is characterized by introjection (avoiding negative consequences) and external regulation (receiving a reward) factors. Results demonstrated autonomy-motivated students participated in synchronous web-conferencing and contributed higher quality and quantity of asynchronous posts. Although Hrastinski (2008) and Giseber et al. (2013) approached their studies quite differently, the results indicate student motivation drives both forms of interaction in online courses.

RECOMMENDATIONS FOR IMPLEMENTATION

Creating methods for quality interactions leading to learning, satisfaction, and a sense of community has been a concern of distance education for decades. Although asynchronous has been the primary method for interacting in the online setting, technological advancements have made it possible for students and instructors to interact in a more face-to-face like setting. This is not to assume asynchronous learning is no longer important or undesirable as a method of interacting; the research indicates both formats play a part in keeping students connected, learning the content, and providing satisfaction in the online classroom. Educators must keep in mind student motivation, especially in interacting with peers and instructors, as an important element in deciding when and how to use both forms of interacting.

Because the findings regarding how and when to implement asynchronous and synchronous interactions were mixed, as well as the methods used to gather, collect, and interpret the data, researchers find it difficult to state whether either interaction is best in the online setting. Several researchers argued asynchronous interactions should be used for group work, especially when content is difficult and requires reflection before posting (Griffith & Graham, 2014; Hrastinski, 2008; Mabrito, 2006). Additionally, Overbaugh and Casiello (2008), Strang (2013), and Rockinson-Szapkiw and Wendt (2015) recommended using synchronous interactions for group projects, because they found the media richness of synchronous tools assisted in the deeper learning process. Other researchers posited synchronous interactions should be used for socializing, planning of activities, and discussing less complex tasks (Duncan et al., 2012; Hrastinski, 2008). These findings can be summarized into the following conclusions: instructors must examine course content, learner motivation and needs, and learning outcomes before deciding on the types of interaction to be woven into course work.

Before making recommendations for how and when to use each type of interaction, however, technical support for online students should be briefly addressed. Ustati and Hassan (2013) noted that just as important as instructor-student support is university support to address issues arising with the technology because of the frustration technical issues can cause. Pan and Sullivan (2005) cautioned instructors not to make the assumption all students are proficient, or even familiar, with online learning platforms. To address this issue, McBrien et al. (2009) recommended initial training with the synchronous platform be implemented before classes begin. Pan and Sullivan (2005) and Giesber et al. (2014) recommended instructors provide technical support to teach students to use the technology for interacting in their courses. If students become frustrated in trying to use the technology, they may not learn the content (Benson & Samarawickerema, 2009; Ustati & Hassan, 2013). McBrien and Jones (2009) also reported when technical issues arose, students experienced more transactional distance, and they believed they had little control over what was occurring in the classroom. These findings are important, as any type of frustration has been demonstrated to increase transactional distance in online learning.

CONCLUSIONS

Even though many studies have been conducted about synchronous and asynchronous interactions, areas remain for future research. As noted earlier, results of recent studies of the quality and quantity of asynchronous and synchronous discussions related to course grades have been inconclusive, and the authors found it prudent to determine how to more effectively use interaction in specifically supporting deeper learning, and subsequently higher grades. As synchronous technology advances, it also might be interesting to see if students predict synchronous interaction will replace asynchronous interaction in the future.

The importance of interactions in the online learning environment have been the subject of much research, and researchers will likely continue the discussion related to positive and negative components of asynchronous and synchronous interactions in online learning environments. Regardless of the format, students report feeling more connected to the online experience, report higher levels of satisfaction, continue to be motivated to engage, and are more successful in group and individual work. Research has provided support for both types, and instructors must take into consideration the motivation and needs of their students, the specific demands of the course content, and the available technical support before deciding what method of interaction is appropriate for their courses.

REFERENCES

Benson, R., & Samarawickrema, G. (2009). Addressing the context of e-learning: Using transactional distance theory to inform design. *Distance Education, 30*(1), 5–21. doi:10.1080/01587910902845972

Benton, S. L., Li, D., & Brown, R. (2014). Transactional distance in online graduate courses at doctoral institutions. *Journal of Online Doctoral Education, 1*(1), 41–55.

Buxton, E. (2014). Pharmacists' perception of synchronous versus asynchronous distance learning for continuing education programs. *American Journal of Pharmaceutical Education, 78*(1), 1–7. doi:10.5688/ajpe7818

Chundur, S., & Prakash, S. (2009). Synchronous vs asynchronous communications—What works best in an online environment? Lessons learnt. In G. Siemens & C. Fulford (Eds.), *EdMedia 2009: World conference on educational multimedia, hypermedia, and telecommunications* (pp. 3541–3545). Chesapeake, VA: Association for the Advancement of Computing in Education.

Dammers, R. J. (2009). Utilizing Internet-based videoconferencing for instrumental music lessons. *Applications of Research in Music Education, 28*(1), 17–24. doi:10.1177/8755123309344159

Duncan, K., Kenworthy, A., & McNamara, R. (2012). The effects of synchronous and asynchronous participation on students' performance in online accounting courses. *Accounting Education, 21*(4), 431–449. doi:10.1080/09639284.2012.673387

Falloon, G. (2011). Making the connection: Moore's theory of transactional distance and its relevance to the use of a virtual classroom in postgraduate online teacher education. *Journal of Research and Technology in Education, 43*(3), 187–209. Retrieved from http://www.anitacrawley.net/Articles/Falloon2011.pdf

Giesbers, B., Rienties, B., Tempelaar, D., & Gijselaers, W. (2014). A dynamic analysis of the interplay between asynchronous and synchronous communication in online learning: The impact of motivation. *Journal of Computer Assisted Learning, 30,* 30–50. doi:10.1111/jcal.12020

Griffiths, M., & Graham, C. R. (2010). Using asynchronous video to achieve instructor immediacy and closeness in online classes: Experience from three cases. *International Journal on E-Learning, 9*(3), 325–340.

Hrastinski, S. (2008). A study of asynchronous and synchronous e-learning methods discovered that each supports different purposes. *Educause Quarterly, 4,* 51–55. Retrieved from http://www.educause.edu/ero/article/asynchronous-and-synchronous-e-learning

Hutti, D. L. G. (2007, March). Online learning, quality, and Illinois community colleges. *MERLOT Journal of Online Learning and Teaching, 3*(1). Retrieved from http://jolt.merlot.org/vol3no1/hutti.pdf

Jones, J. G., Morales, C., & Knezek, G. A. (2005). 3-dimensional online learning environments: Examining attitudes toward information technology between students in Internet-based 3-dimensional and face-to-face classroom instruction. *Educational Media International, 42*(3), 219–236.

Mabrito, M. (2006). A study of synchronous versus asynchronous collaboration in an online business writing class. *The American Journal of Distance Education, 20*(2), 93–107.

McBrien, J. L., Jones, P., & Cheng, R. (2009). Virtual spaces: Employing a synchronous online classroom to facilitate student engagement in online learning. *The International Review of Research in Open and Distributed Learning, 10*(3). Retrieved from http://www. irrodl.org/index.php/irrodl/article/view/605/1264

Moore, M. G. (1973). Toward a theory of independent learning and teaching. *Journal of Higher Education, 44*(12), 661–679.

Moore, M. G. (1989). Editorial: Three types of interaction. *American Journal of Distance Education, 3*(2), 1–7.

Overbaugh, R. C., & Casiello, A. R. (2008). Distributed collaborative problem-based graduate-level learning: Students' perspectives on communication tool selection and efficacy. *Computers in Human Behavior, 24*(2008), 497–515. doi:10.1016/j.chb.2007.02.017

Pan, C., & Sullivan, M. (2005). Promoting synchronous interaction in an eLearning environment. *Technical Horizons in Education Journal, 33*(2), 27–30. Retrieved from http://thejournal.com/Articles/2005/09/01/Promoting-Synchronous-Interaction-in-an--eLearning-Environment.aspx

Rockinson-Szapkiw, A., & Wendt, J. (2015). Technologies that assist in online group work: A comparison of synchronous and asynchronous computer mediated communication technologies on students' learning and community. *Journal of Educational Multimedia and Hypermedia, 24*(3), 263–279.

Schullo, S., Hilbelink, A., Venable, M., & Barron, A. E. (2007). Selecting a virtual classroom system: Elluminate Live vs. Macromedia Breeze (Adobe Acrobat Connect Professional). *MERLOT Journal of Online Learning and Teaching, 3*(4), 331–345. Retrieved from http://jolt.merlot.org/documents/hilbelink.pdf

Stein, D. S., Wanstreet, C. E., & Calvin, J. (2009). How a novice adult online learner experiences transactional distance. *The Quarterly Review of Distance Education, 10*(3), 305–311. Retrieved from http://eric.ed.gov/?id=EJ889334

Stein, D. S., Wanstreet, C. E., Calvin, J., Overtoom, C., & Wheaton, J. E. (2005). Bridging the transactional distance gap in online learning environments. *The American Journal of Distance Education, 19*(2), 105–118.

Strang, K. (2013). Cooperative learning in graduate student projects: Comparing synchronous versus asynchronous collaboration. *Journal of Interactive Learning Research, 24*(4), 447–464.

Ustati, R., & Hassan, S. S. S. (2013). Distance learning students' need: Evaluating interactions from Moore's theory of transactional distance. *Turkish Online Journal of Distance Education, 14*(2), 292–304. Retrieved from http://eric.ed.gov/?id=EJ1013753

KEY COMPONENTS
OF ONLINE GROUP PROJECTS
Faculty Perceptions

Christine E. Wade and Bruce A. Cameron
University of Wyoming

Kari Morgan
Kansas State University

Karen C. Williams
University of Wyoming

In order to better understand faculty perceptions of group work, a survey was deployed to online teaching instructors. Results suggest that most faculty find student socialization (e.g., being supportive, caring about each other), communication, reliability, and dependability important in the group process. However, very few faculty rated the development of deeper interpersonal relationships as very important. Finally, most faculty said it was important for group members to have a role, though most suggested group roles were decided upon by group members. Implications for group project implementation are discussed.

INTRODUCTION

The ability to work effectively in a group was recently rated as one of the top two skills employers are currently looking for in job candidates (National Association of Colleges and Employers, 2016). Further, according to the National Leadership Council for Liberal Education and America's Promise (2007), one of the "essential learning outcomes" of a college degree is intellectual and practical skills, which includes teamwork and problem solving (p. 7). Group projects have been touted as a unique opportunity to practice teamwork skills, create and refine interpersonal communication skills, and develop a deeper understanding of course content and concepts (Chapman, Meuter, Toy, & Wright, 2010; Chapman & Van Auken, 2001; Kendall, 1999; Myers et al., 2009). Further, group work

• **Christine E. Wade**, associate professor of family and consumer sciences, University of Wyoming. Telephone: (307) 766-4011. E-mail: cwade@uwyo.edu • **Bruce A. Cameron**, associate professor of family and consumer sciences, University of Wyoming. Telephone: (307) 766-4145. E-mail: unsw@uwyo.edu • **Kari Morgan**, associate professor of family studies and human services, Kansas State University. Telephone: (785) 532-1476. E-mail: kmmorgan@k-state.edu • **Karen C. Williams**, professor emeritus of family and consumer sciences, University of Wyoming. E-mail: cachevki@uwyo.edu

The Quarterly Review of Distance Education, Volume 17(1), 2016, pp. 33–41
Copyright © 2016 Information Age Publishing, Inc.
ISSN 1528-3518

opportunities in online classes provide an opportunity to create a community of learners, which has been associated with increased student satisfaction and level of learning (e.g., Dawson, 2006; Ouzts, 2006; Rovai, 2002; Rovai & Barnum, 2003; Sullivan, 2002). Researchers have often suggested that behaviors fostering connectedness, including developing interpersonal relationships with group members, enhance a sense of community within the group (e.g., Rovai, 2002).

Studies supporting the importance of the development of interpersonal relationships suggest that faculty should scaffold group projects through team-building exercises, synchronous group meetings, social icebreakers, and shared social support systems, so as to foster the development of interpersonal relationships (e.g., Bonk, Wisher, & Nigrelli, 2004; Wade, Cameron, Morgan, & Williams, 2011; Young & Henquinet, 2000). However, little is currently known about faculty perceptions of the importance of interpersonal relationship development between students within group work settings (Chapman et al., 2010). This is a critical gap in the literature, as it has large implications for how faculty facilitate student group processes.

To date, only a few studies have examined faculty perceptions of group work (e.g., August, Hurtado, Wimsatt & Dey, 2002; Chapman et al., 2010; Sinclair, 1997). Sinclair (1997) found that although job recruiters ranked the ability to work in team as the third most important skill of a potential employee, faculty only ranked it eighth. Chapman et al. (2010) found that students tended to feel more positive about their group's dynamics, cohesion, trust, and conflict resolution abilities, and also their ability to learn through group work, than did faculty. Finally, August and colleagues (2002) found that a majority of students and faculty both reported that collaborative/cooperative learning assisted the learning experience.

However, this very limited literature examining faculty perceptions of group work has not explored online group settings. This is a

critical gap, as distance education enrollments continue to increase, and the demand for innovation and best practice in these courses is real (Fish & Wickersham, 2009). For example, the U.S. Department of Education reported that the number of students taking distance education classes rose from 8 to 26% from 2000 to 2012 (U.S. Department of Education, 2014). Further, according to Meyer (2010), "There are more global virtual teams today than ever before. And their numbers are increasing rapidly" (Meyer, 2010, para. 2). Thus, understanding how to best foster group work in an online educational setting is crucial so as to develop necessary teamwork skills in students. Examining faculty perceptions of group work occurring online is an important first step toward gaining this understanding.

METHOD

Survey Instrument

The current study utilized the survey instrument shown in the appendix. This survey is a modified version of Wade et al.'s (2011) survey of student perceptions of online group work, altered in order to assess faculty perceptions by rewording questions so that the topic remained the same but the wording was appropriate for the perspective of the faculty member instead of the participating student. The faculty survey contained 17 demographic questions and 33 questions regarding group work design, processes, experiences, and dynamics. Response options for questions regarding group work were answered on a 4-point Likert scale, with answer options ranging from "very important" to "unnecessary" or "strongly agree" to "strongly disagree."

Participants

The survey was deployed at a Western university across two semesters via e-mail invitation to all instructors of online classes; therefore, course content, length, and design likely varied greatly among respondents. A total of 46 instructors responded. The average age of respondents was 49.6 years, 93% identified their race/ethnicity as Caucasian, and 54% were female. Only instructors who have/do include group work in their courses continued on to the group work questions. For those who have/do include group projects (n = 30), the average age was 52 years, 93% identified their race/ethnicity as Caucasian, and 63% were female. The majority of respondents identified themselves as adjuncts or assistant lecturers (60%), reported they had taught more than 4 online courses (69%), and the majority of group projects were four weeks or less in duration (75%).

RESULTS

Importance of Process, Experience, and Group Dynamics

The majority of faculty who indicated using group projects in their online courses (86.2% or higher) agreed or strongly agreed with the importance of the process and experience questions (Questions 18–27 and 29). Similarly, the majority of faculty (97% or higher) agreed or strongly agreed with the importance of all but one group dynamic questions (Questions 33–36). The one exception was the question regarding the importance of students developing deep relationships with online group members, to which only 40.7% of responding faculty agreed or strongly agreed. Faculty also tended to support the importance of etiquette in group projects (90% or higher agreed or strongly agreed; Questions 48 and 50).

Faculty were more divided, though, on questions regarded group experiences. Most faculty agreed or strongly agreed with the importance of developing supportive relationships with group members and developing a sense of trust with group members (96.3% and 100% respectively), and a slightly lower percentage but still majority agreed or strongly

agreed with the importance of students getting to know their group members on a personal level, developing specific roles in their groups, and identifying specific characteristics of their group members (63.0%, 78.6%, and 73.0% respectively). However, a minority of faculty agreed or strongly agreed that it is important for students to develop deep relationships with their group members (40.7%).

Group Roles

Of the 27 faculty who answered the question, most suggested group roles are typically decided upon by the group members (i.e., by group members either through purposeful or accidental assignment; 88%) instead of by the instructor (11%). Despite a lack of faculty involvement in the assigning of group roles, faculty did seem to endorse the importance of most group roles (leader, 79%; facilitator, 79%; editor, 79%; cheerleader/supporter, 67%; presenter, 75%; writer, 83%; and researcher, 96%). However a minority of faculty felt that the role of liaison to the instructor was important (46%).

Group Trust

Question 45 asked faculty to indicate what they think contributed to a lack of trust when noted in an online group. Of the 22 faculty who responded, the most common responses were that group members did not complete tasks on time (68%), group members did not work as promised (72%), and group members did not participate in planning sessions (64%). Only a minority indicated that not being able to meet face to face (4.5%) or group members not being clear about expectations (14%) contributed to the lack of trust.

Group Member Qualities

Faculty were asked to rank the top 5 characteristics they believed are important for students to identify in other online group members. Faculty ranked their most important quality with a 1, their second most important quality a 2, and so forth up to a maximum of 5. Scores given to each characteristic were then reverse coded, in order to weight each score. In other words, a characteristic ranked a 1 was recoded into a score of 5 (thus having the most weight), a ranking of 2 was recoded into a 4, et cetera. These weighted scores were then summed across all respondents to form a weighted total for each characteristic. Two characteristics, reliability and dependability, rose to the top and received weighted total scores of 73 and 79 respectively (the next closest score was 54). The lowest weighted characteristic sum score was 25 for providing feedback.

Faculty also ranked their top five etiquette behaviors for online group interactions. Rankings were transformed into weighted sums in the same way as described above. Two etiquette behaviors, reliable and regular communication (both with weighted sums of 73), rose above the others (with the next weighted sum of 41). The lowest etiquette behaviors (with weighted sum scores of 12) were avoiding conflict and being a good listener.

DISCUSSION

Reports from company executives confirm that teamwork skills are critical in today's job applicants (Vance, 2007). Understanding how to work with others toward a common goal is a skill that needs to be developed in today's college students. Therefore, group projects in college settings that allow the development of these skills seem critical to developing students who are competitive in today's workplace market.

On the whole, this study found that faculty endorsed the importance of most of the process, experience, and group dynamics questions. That is, faculty seem to feel that when students work in online groups, they should get to know their group members, work together in a supportive manner, play nice (e.g., being

supportive, caring about each other), and communicate (including asking questions, dealing with conflict, and giving feedback). However, most faculty did not feel it was important for students to develop deep relationships with their group members. This is interesting, as previous research has often suggested that developing deeper relationships within a group is crucial to developing a sense of trust, which then affects the success of the group (e.g., Jarvenpaa, Knoll, & Leidner, 1998; Keyton, 2000; Preece, 2000; Smith, 2008). In fact, Keyton (2000) states that, "Group member relationship development and maintenance are the primary processes that enhance or detract from how group work is carried out" (p. 387). This area of research would be worth exploring further to allow for a better understanding of the importance of developing relationships in online group settings, as well as how faculty can best support these relationships (if they are determined to be important to the success of the group).

A further important point is that although interpersonal relationships may be necessary to develop trust and successfully complete the group project, it may indeed be the case that, in the typical short duration of group work, interpersonal relationships are not necessary (Jarvenpaa et al., 1998; Liu, Magjuka, Bonk, & Lee, 2007; Mayer, Davis, & Schoorman, 1995). Because many faculty and students never participate in longer term projects, this particular aspect of group work might never become important in their experiences. Instead, it may only be in much longer projects (i.e., longer than 2 months; Jarvenpaa et al., 1998) that interpersonal relationships become critical to the success of the group. As the majority of faculty responding to this survey indicated their group projects lasted 4 weeks or less, this may explain why these faculty placed less importance on developing interpersonal relationships. Future research examining both the actual and perceived importance of interpersonal relationship development over varying lengths of time (i.e., weeks to months or longer) is needed in order to test the accuracy of this assumption.

With regard to group member roles, the majority of faculty indicated that group members determined role allocation within the group. Faculty also agreed that there are many roles that are important for an online group to take on, and that they are typically able to identify within a group who has taken on each of these roles. Finally, and as expected, faculty's perceptions of what tended to result in the breakdown of trust within a group (i.e., group members not completing tasks on time, group members not working as promised, and group members not participating in planning sessions) fit well with the characteristics they felt were important for students to identify within other group members (i.e., reliability and dependability) and the most important group etiquette behaviors (reliability and regular communication). Thus, not only do faculty feel it is important that group members need to develop a sense of trust in their group and trust group members to complete tasks, but they also feel that reliability, dependability, and communication are critical and that the breakdown of these aspects then lead to a breakdown in group trust.

IMPLICATIONS FOR TEACHING

Although this study was completed by only a small number of self-selecting faculty who teach online classes that contain a group project, and therefore generalizations must be made cautiously, these findings have a few important implications for teaching. First, faculty opinions on the importance of socialization activities (e.g., getting to know their group members, being supportive, caring about each other, communicating, dealing with conflict, being reliable and dependable) may be an important issue for faculty to consider as they develop their group work assignments. Faculty often assume that students also see this as important and are capable of engaging in basic socialization tasks (Chapman & Van Auken,

2001). This could lead, however, to students sensing from their instructors that socialization tasks are not important (as there is never an explicit mention of them) and/or group members not knowing how to go about these tasks (as no scaffolding was provided). In fact, Chapman et al. (2010) found that faculty tended to underrate the personal interest students took in each other. Thus, faculty should consider explicitly discussing, encouraging, and supporting student socialization before and during online group work.

Faculty also tended to agree that there are many roles that are important for an online group to take on; however, these roles are typically assigned by group members. Allowing students to assign their roles in and of itself may not be problematic. However, as discussed above, if there are important roles to be assigned and these roles are not specifically identified, defined, and told to be assigned to group members, students may not know what roles are important, may not realize that explicitly assigning roles will help their group function more effectively, and/or may not think the instructor feels that group role assignment is important. Thus creating initial assignments that help students understand and assign group roles prior to the start of a group project may ensure group success.

Finally, since faculty members seem to have a consensus about what often leads to a breakdown of trust within a group (i.e., group members not completing tasks on time, group members not working as promised, and group members not participating in planning sessions), it is also important to have a mechanism through which specific group members are held accountable. Recommendations include:

- Encourage and/or require groups to make a list of all project tasks and a timeline of when those tasks will be completed.
- Make group member participation visible through the use of group planning threads or chat rooms so that individual student

participation and group functioning can be monitored.

• Provide a place (such as a document share) where group members post drafts, handouts, presentation materials, et cetera, to help make participation and timeliness visible to the instructor as well as other group members.

• Design the assignment so that individuals are held accountable to their group. For example, include a participation component to the final grade that is individually assigned to each student. These participation points can then be affected by mechanisms such as the ones above, and/or by allowing students to provide feedback about their fellow group members (see Williams, Cameron, & Morgan (2012) for a complete description).

Acknowledgment: This research was supported in part by a grant from the University of Wyoming Outreach School.

REFERENCES

August, L., Hurtado, S., Wimisatt, L.A., & Dey, E. L. (2002, June). *Learning styles: Student preferences vs. faculty perceptions.* Presented at the annual forum for the Association for Institutional Research, Toronto, Ontario, Canada.

Bonk, C. J., Wisher, R. A., & Nigrelli, M. L. (2004). Learning communities, communities of practice: Principles, technologies, and examples. In K. Littleton, D. Miell, & D. Faulkner (Eds.), *Learning to collaborate, collaborating to learn* (pp. 199–219). New York, NY: Nova Science.

Chapman, K. J., Meuter, M. L., Toy, D., & Wright, L. K. (2010). Are student groups dysfunctional? Perspectives from both sides of the classroom. *Journal of Marketing Education, 32*(1), 39–49. doi:10.1177/0273475309335575

Chapman, K. J., & Van Auken, S. (2001). Creating positive group project experiences: An examination of the role of the instructor on students' perceptions of group projects. *Journal of Marketing Education, 23*(2), 117–127. doi:10.1177/0273475301232005

Dawson, S. (2006). A study of the relationship between student communication interaction and sense of community. *The Internet and Higher Education, 9*(3), 153–162. doi:10.1016/j.iheduc.2006.06.007

Fish, W. W., & Wickersham, L. E. (2009). Best practices for online instructors: Reminders. *Quarterly Review of Distance Education, 10*(3), 279–284

Jarvenpaa, S. L., Knoll, K., & Leidner, D. (1998). Is anybody out there? Antecedents of trust in global virtual teams. *Journal of Management Information Systems, 14*(4), 29–64. Retrieved from http://www.jmis-web.org

Kendall, M. E. (1999). Let students do the work. *College Teaching, 47,* 84–87. doi:10.1080/87567559909595791

Keyton, J. (2000). The relational side of groups. *Small Group Research, 31*(4), 387–396. doi:10.1177/104649640003100401

Liu, X., Magjuka, R. J., Bonk, C. J., & Lee, S. (2007). Does sense of community matter? An examination of participants' perceptions of building learning communities in online courses. *Quarterly Review of Distance Education, 8*(1), 9–24. Retrieved from http://www.infoagepub.com/quarterly-review-of-distance-education.html

Mayer, R. C., Davis, J. H., & Schoorman, F. D. (1995). An integrative model of organizational trust. *Academy of Management Review, 20*(3), 709–734. Retrieved from http://www.jstor.org/action/showPublication?journalCode=acadmanarevi

Meyer, E. (2010, August 19). The four keys to success with virtual teams [Online post]. *Forbes.* Retrieved from http://www.forbes.com/2010/08/19/virtual-teams-meetings-leadership-managing-cooperation.html

Myers, S. A., Bogdan, L. M., Eidsness, M. A., Johnson, A. N., Shoo, M. E., Smith, N. A., … Zackery, B. A. (2009). Taking a trait approach to understanding college students' perceptions of group work. *College Student Journal, 43*(3), 822–831. Retrieved from http://search.proquest.com/docview/236525167/fulltext/139F43494147A461AAE/17?accountid=14793

National Association of Colleges and Employers. (2016). *Job outlook 2016.* Retrieved from http://www.naceweb.org/surveys/job-outlook.aspx.

National Leadership Council for Liberal Education and America's Promise. (2007). *College learning for the new global century.* Retrieved from

https://www.aacu.org/sites/default/files/files/
LEAP/GlobalCentury_final.pdf

Preece, J. (2000). *Online communities: Designing usability, supporting sociability.* New York, NY: Wiley.

Ouzts, K. (2006). Sense of community in online courses. *Quarterly Review of Distance Education, 7*(3), 285–296. Retrieved from http://www.infoagepub.com/quarterly-review-of-distance-education.html

Rovai, A. P. (2002). Sense of community, perceived cognitive learning, and persistence in asynchronous learning networks. *The Internet and Higher Education, 5*(4), 319–332. doi:10.1016/S1096-7516(02)00130-6

Rovai, A. P., & Barnum, K. T. (2003). On-line course effectiveness: An analysis of student interactions and perceptions of learning. *Journal of Distance Education, 18*(1), 57–73. Retrieved from http://www.jofde.ca/index.php/jde/index

Sinclair, K. E. (1997). Workforce competencies of college graduates. In H. F. O'Neil (Ed.), *Workforce readiness: Competencies and assessment* (pp. 103–120). Mahwah, NJ: Erlbaum.

Smith, R. O. (2008). The paradox of trust in online collaborative groups. *Distance Education, 29*(3), 325–340. doi:10.1080/01587910802395839

Sullivan, P. (2002). It's easier to be yourself when you are invisible: Female college students discuss their online experiences. *Innovative Higher Education, 27*(2), 129–144. Retrieved from http://www.springer.com/education+%26+language/higher+education/journal/10755

U.S. Department of Education. (2014). *Enrollment in distance education courses by state: Fall 2012* (NCES Publication No. 2014-023). Retrieved from https://nces.ed.gov/pubsearch/pubsinfo.asp?pubid=2014023

Vance, E. (2007). College graduates lack key skills, report says. *Chronicle of Higher Education, 53*(22), A30. Retrieved from http://chronicle.com/article/College-Graduates-Lack-Key/33993/

Wade, C. E., Cameron, B. A., Morgan, K., & Williams, K. C. (2011). Online group projects: Are interpersonal relationships necessary for developing trust? *Distance Education, 32*(3), 383–396.

Williams, K. C., Cameron, B. A., & Morgan, K. (2012). Supporting online group projects. *North American College Teachers of Agriculture Journal, 56*, 15–20.

Young, C. B., & Henquinet, J. A. (2000). A conceptual framework for designing group projects. *Journal of Education for Business, 76*(1), 56–60. doi:10.1080/08832320009599051

APPENDIX: GROUP PROJECTS SURVEY FOR FACULTY

Demographic Information

1. What is your age?
2. What is your race or ethnicity?
3. What is your sex?
4. What is your faculty status?
5. In what college do you teach?
6. Including this course, how many online classes have you taught?
7. Do you read journal articles regarding online teaching?
8. Have you attended any trainings, workshops, or conferences regarding online teaching?
9. Of the online classes you have taught previously, including your current class, how many have included a group project?

No Group Projects
10. If you do not utilize group projects in your online classes, why? Are there barriers, problems, and/or concerns that keep you from utilizing group projects?

Information about Group Projects
11. If you do utilize group projects in your online courses, why? What do you see as the benefits?
12. What has gone smoothly or worked well with your online group projects?
13. What has been problematic with your online group projects?
14. What level(s) of courses do you teach online that include a group project? Please check all that apply. (answer choices: freshman, sophomore, junior, senior, graduate)
15. What are the typical durations of your online group projects? Please check all that apply. (answer choices: Less than 1

week, 1–2 weeks, 3–4 weeks, 1–2 months, longer than 2 months)

16. Have you seen differences in how online groups perform based on the duration of the project? If so, please explain.

17. Would you be willing to participate in a focus group regarding online group projects? If so, please provide us with your e-mail address.

Process and Experience

(Answer choices to Questions 18-27, 29: strongly agree, agree, disagree, strongly disagree)

18. It is important that group members care about each other.

19. It is important for online group members to encourage each other to ask questions.

20. It is important for students to be able to rely on other online group members.

21. It is important for online group members to connect with one another.

22. It is important for group members to communicate frequently.

23. It is important for online group members to trust each other to complete assigned tasks.

24. It is important for online group members to be supportive of one another.

25. It is important for online groups to exhibit a sense of community.

26. It is important for differences of opinion within online groups to be successfully negotiated by the group members themselves.

27. It is important for online groups to be a cohesive unit.

28. When working with an online group project, I encourage my students to meet … (Answer choices: face to face, through online threads, in an online chat room, using web casting, by voice [phone, Bluetooth, etc.], using Skype, using social networking tools [Facebook, wikis, blogs, etc.], not applicable)

29. It is important for online group members to provide constructive feedback to each other when communicating.

Group Dynamics

(Answer choices to Questions 33-37: strongly agree, agree, disagree, strongly disagree)

30. What do you see as your role in facilitating online group work?

31. Do you facilitate online group roles or creating a sense of community within the online groups? Why or why not?

32. Does your level of facilitation change based on the level of the course? If so, how?

33. It is important for groups to develop goals regarding the online group project.

34. It is important for students to make their expectations for the online group known.

35. It is important that students invest at an interpersonal level with online group members.

36. It is important for students to provide feedback about processes associated with the online group project.

37. It is important for students to develop deep relationships with the online group members.

Importance of Experience

(Answer choices to Questions 38, 39, 43, 44, 47: very important, important, not important, unnecessary)

38. How important is it that students get to know each other on a personal level in online group work?

39. How important is it for students to develop specific roles in online groups?

40. Are you typically able to identify the roles students have taken in their online groups? (answer choices: yes, no)

41. How are roles typically assigned in your online groups? (answer choices: by me, by a group member[s], created as individual group members volunteered, created by group agreement, seemed to "just happen," other —please specify).

42. What role(s) do you feel are important for students to fill in online group work? Please check all that apply. (answer choices: leader, facilitator, editor, cheer-

leader/supporter, presenter, writer, liaison with instructor, researcher, other—please specify)

43. How important is it for students to develop supportive relationships with their online group members?

44. How important is it for students to develop a sense of trust with their online group members?

45. If you have perceived a lack of trust in an online group, what do you think contributed to that lack of trust? Please check all that apply. (answer choices: group members were not able to meet face to face, group members did not answer questions when posed, group members did not complete tasks on time, group members did not do work as promised, group members did not participate in planning sessions, group members were not clear about expectations, other—please specify)

46. What are the top five characteristics you believe it is important that students identify in other online group members? Below is a list of characteristics. While many may be important to you, please select ONLY your top five, and indicate which is the most important, with 1 being the most important to you, 2 being the second most important, et cetera. Again, please select only your top five. (answer choices: knowledge about the subject, reliability, dependability, honesty, respectful, provides feedback, follow through, work ethic, organized, positive attitude)

47. How important is it for students to identify specific characteristics of their online group members?

Group Etiquette

(Answer choices to Questions 48, 50: very important, important, not important, unnecessary)

48. How important is it that ground rules be developed for online group interactions?

49. Please select the 5 most important group etiquette behaviors in order of their importance to group performance. Below is a list of behaviors. While many may be important to you, please select ONLY your top five, and indicate which is the most important, with 1 being the most important to you, 2 being the second most important, et cetera. Again, please select only your top five. (answer choices: politeness, avoiding conflict, showing care and concern for others, reliability, follow through, trustworthiness, regular communication, good listener, positive attitude)

50. How important is it that online group members contribute to etiquette within the group?

BLENDED VERSUS TRADITIONAL COURSE DELIVERY
Comparing Students' Motivation, Learning Outcomes, and Preferences

Hungwei Tseng and Eamonn Joseph Walsh, Jr.
Jacksonville State University

This study sought to compare and assess students' experiences and perceptions in a blended and a traditional course, as well as their level of learning motivation, level of learning outcomes and skills, and learning achievement. Two instructors who were teaching 1 section of an undergraduate English literacy course using the face-to-face format while, in the same semester, teaching another section of the same class in a hybrid/blended format were willing to invite students (blended: $n = 26$; traditional: $n = 26$) to participate in this study. Students in the blended course reported significantly higher overall learning motivation ($p = .045$) than students in the traditional course. They also reported higher levels of learning outcomes ($p = .45$) and final grades ($p = .192$) with no significant difference. Moreover, blended learners indicated that they would like to take more blended classes and would recommend them to their friends.

INTRODUCTION

In the early 21st century, the integration of synchronous or asynchronous learning technologies provided instructors with innovative ways to deliver learning content and activities. Thus, online learning or distance learning has emerged as a significant and viable method of course delivery in higher education. Research has found that online learning systems can provide personalized and adaptive instruction that can be creatively customized to suit individual capabilities and learning styles (Al-Khanjari, 2014; Downes, 2005) and also engage students (Cho & Cho, 2014; Sydnor, Sass, Adeola, & Snuggs, 2014) in active learning with interac-

• **Hungwei Tseng**, Instructional Designer, Office of Teaching, Learning, & Technology and assistant professor, Department of Educational Resources, Jacksonville State University, 700 Pelham Rd. N, 212A Self Hall, Jacksonville, AL 36256-1602. Telephone: (256) 782-8529. E-mail: htseng@jsu.edu • **Eamonn Joseph Walsh, Jr.**, Associate Vice President, Office of Teaching, Learning, & Technology, Jacksonville State University, 700 Pelham Rd. N, 212A Self Hall, Jacksonville, AL 36256-1602. Telephone: (256) 782-8172 E-mail: ejwalsh@jsu.edu

The Quarterly Review of Distance Education, Volume 17(1), 2016, pp. 43–52
ISSN 1528-3518

tive materials and resources. However, some strengths of face-to-face learning from the social constructivist perspective (e.g., level of human connection, social interaction, and comment spontaneity) are often deficient or even unavailable in online learning environments (Bonk & Graham, 2006; Woo & Reeves, 2007). Consequently, it is important for educators to take such deficiencies into account when considering the most effective and appropriate methods of delivering instruction.

Blended learning (BL) is one of the various methods being adopted to deliver meaningful learning experiences (Lim & Morris, 2009) and is found to be effective in addressing diverse learning styles (Bielawski & Metcalf, 2003). Saeed, Yang, and Sinnappan (2009) noted that "today's learners are flexible in stretching their learning styles and are able to accommodate varying instructional strategies, including the use of emerging web technologies" (p. 106). In other words, instructors can apply various instructional strategies and add innovative uses of technology to generate new opportunities for personalized and creative learning. Students know how to seek support and have abilities to resolve learning difficulties associated with uses of technology. Learning materials and resources delivered via different multimedia formats and a combination of technology-facilitated activities may provide mechanisms to accommodate student learning style more consistently in higher education. In addition, BL can foster social interaction, increase access to knowledge, and increase the amount of teacher presence (Osguthorpe & Graham, 2003). In fact, educators have predicted that BL will become the "new normal" in higher education course delivery (Norberg, Dziuban, & Moskal, 2011). According to Heinze and Proctor (2004), blended learning is defined as "learning that is facilitated by the effective combination of different modes of delivery, models of teaching and styles of learning, and founded on transparent communication amongst all parties involved with a course" (p. 12). The blended

course design involves thoughtful integration of various course delivery methods, learning principles, and instructional technologies that can provide learners with a flexible, autonomic, and situated learning environment. Driscoll (2002) identified four approaches that clearly explain the concepts of blended learning:

1. to combine or mix modes of web-based technology (e.g., live virtual classroom, self-paced instruction, collaborative learning, streaming video, audio, and text) to accomplish an educational goal;
2. to combine various pedagogical approaches (e.g., constructivism, behaviorism, cognitivism) to produce an optimal learning outcome with or without instructional technology;
3. to combine any form of instructional technology (e.g., videotape, CD-ROM, web-based training, film) with face-to-face instructor-led training; and
4. to mix or combine instructional technology with actual job tasks in order to create a harmonious effect of learning and working (p. 1).

In the first decade of blended learning research, researchers have been exploring and experimenting with BL in the instructional and practical aspects, across discipline and context, and at a single-course and institutionalwide levels. Halverson, Graham, Spring, and Drysdale (2012) conducted a thematic analysis to search for the center of this emerging area of BL studies and concluded that BL research covers the topics in instructional design, disposition, exploration, learner outcomes, comparison, technology, and interaction. Aspden and Helm (2004) explored student engagement and interaction in the context of a blended environment and reported that a blended approach facilitates connections and engagement between students and the other aspects of their learning experience. The findings in Riffel and Sibley's (2005) study revealed that the blended course format was better or equivalent to the traditional course and students showed more evidence of learning gains. Current research has centered on comparing student achievement between blended and traditional learning environment. Melton, Graf, and Chopak-Foss (2009) compared student achievement in sections of the traditional health course ($n = 153$) and the blended health course ($n = 98$) during fall 2007. The results revealed that final course grade was significantly higher ($p = 0.048$) for blended students ($M = 79.62$) than traditional students ($M = 76.38$). They concluded that students in a blended course are more responsible for learning content on their own time; thus, in-class time can be applied to scaffold for deeper engagements through active learning and authentic tasks. In addition, a statistically significant difference in students' achievement was found between blended learning and classroom learning in Al-Qahtani and Higgins's (2013) study. The authors noted that blended learning environment integrates face-to-face teaching featuring the presence of an instructor and e-learning with flexibility and accessibility on learning process. This course delivery method gives students opportunities to share control of learning and to adapt to different learning context and situations.

Motivation in Blended Learning Environments

While these findings support the positive effect of blended learning, there is a lack of research on students' level of learning motivation and how students can be motivated in blended learning environments (Rovai & Downey, 2010). According to Clayton, Blumberg, and Auld (2010), motivation is still an important factor in learning despite the developing of innovative ways to deliver instruction. Prior research (Ames & Archer, 1988; Meece, Blumenfeld, & Hoyle, 1988) found that students with a motivational orientation involving beliefs that the task is interesting and important will engage in more metacognitive activity and more effective effort management. Moreover, So and Brush (2008) argued that in

blended learning environments, the importance of students' self-motivation and self-management increases because there is less in-class time and more emphasis on self-regulated learning. Hence, there is a need to better understand the principles of motivation and the extent to which it influences teaching and learning. To investigate students' motivation to learn in blended and traditional learning environments, Keller's (1987a, 1987b) ARCS (attention, relevance, confidence and satisfaction) model of motivation was adopted for this study. The ARCS model includes four categories: (1) Attention: gaining and sustaining attention in relation to the instructional content; (2) Relevance: relating to the learning objective and to the use in future learning; (3) Confidence: building confidence in learning and accomplishment with success occasions; 4) Satisfaction: reinforcing learning satisfaction intrinsically and extrinsically. The ARCS model has been recognized as "the only coherent and comprehensive instructional design model accommodating motivation" (Means, Jonassen, & Dwyer, 1997, p. 5). Only a few studies have used the ARCS model in blended learning environment to examine learning motivation (Gabrielle, 2003; Kim & Keller, 2008). In addition, there is a lack of experimental research on the use of the ARCS model in comparing students' learning motivation among different delivery methods (traditional classroom, e-learning, and blended learning).

Purpose of the Study

This study sought to compare and assess students' experiences and perceptions in a blended and a traditional course, as well as their level of learning motivation, level of learning outcomes and skills, and learning achievement. The research questions that guided the investigation are:

- Research Question 1: Is there a statistically significant difference between students who participated in a blended course and those who participated in a traditional course on their level of learning motivation?

- Research Question 2: Is there a statistically significant difference between students who participated in a blended course and those who participated in a traditional course on their level of learning outcomes and skills?
- Research Question 3: Is there a statistically significant difference between students who participated in a blended course and those who participated in a traditional course on their learning achievement?
- Research Question 4: What are students' perceptions toward blended course delivery method?

METHOD

Sample Selection

Purposive sampling strategies were used to select the participants of this study. Instructors who were teaching one section of an undergraduate class using the face-to-face format while, in the same semester (Spring 2015), teaching another section of the same class in a hybrid/blended format were identified. Two instructors who were teaching undergraduate English literacy courses met the criteria and were willing to invite students to participate in this study. Overall, 26 students from two blended courses completed the survey and there were 13 male (50%) and 13 female (50%) participants. The majority of them ($n = 14$, 53.8%) reported being under 20 years of age and all participants were enrolled as full time. In terms of online learning experience, 11 participants (42.3%) had previously participated in 1 to 5 fully online courses. In addition, most of the participants ($n = 19$, 73.1%) had participated in 1 to 5 blended courses.

Among traditional students from the two courses, 18 male (69.2%) and 8 female (30.7%) completed the surveys. The majority of them ($n = 16$, 57.1%) reported being under 20 years of age and 25 participants were enrolled as full time. In addition, 11 partici-

pants (42.3%) had previously participated in 1 to 5 fully online courses and 15 participants (57.7%) had participated in 1 to 5 blended courses.

Instrumentation

Course Interest Survey (CIS). Keller and Subhiyah's (1993) Course Interest Survey was adapted to measure learning motivation and includes 34 Likert-type items ranging from 1 (*not true*) to 5 (*very true*). The survey was designed using the ARCS model (attention, relevance, confidence, and satisfaction) as the theoretical foundation (Keller, 1987a, 1987b). Attention and confidence subscales have eight items each, while relevance and satisfaction subscales have nine items each. Example survey items include "The instructor knows how to make us feel enthusiastic about the subject matter of this course," "Whether or not I succeed in this course is up to me," and "The content of this course related to my expectations and goals."

Learning Outcomes and Skills Assessment Scale. The 4-item scale designed by Chen and Jones (2007) was adapted and utilized to assess students' skills commonly named as desirable for development in university curricula, including writing, analytical, interpersonal, and computer skills. All items are measured on a 5-point Likert scale, ranging from 1 (*strongly disagree*) to 5 (*strongly agree*). Example survey items include "My writing skills have improved as a result of this class," and "My analytical skills have improved as a result of this class."

Delivery Mode Perceptions Scale. The 9-item scale was developed by the researchers of this study. Its purpose was to investigate students' perceptions toward the blended course delivery method. Example survey items include "The flexibility of hybrid classes allows me to complete assignments on my own time," "The quality of hybrid classes is NOT as good as face-to-face classes," and "I would recommend hybrid classes to my friends."

TABLE 1
Demographic and Courses Taken Information of Participants

	Course Delivery Format	
	Blended (n = 26)	*Traditional (n = 26)*
Gender		
Female	13 (50%)	18 (69.2%)
Male	13 (50%)	8 (30.7%)
Age		
Under 20	14 (53.8%)	15 (57.7%)
20-24	9 (34.6%)	8 (30.7%)
25-29	1 (3.8%)	1 (3.8%)
30-39	2 (7.7%)	
40-49		
Over 50		2 (7.7%)
Enrollment Status		
Full Time	26 (100%)	25 (96.2%)
Part Time		1 (3.8%)
Completed Online Courses		
None	12 (46.2%)	15 (57.7%)
1-5	11 (42.3%)	11 (42.3%)
6-10	1 (3.8%)	
More than 10	2 (7.7%)	
Completed Blended Courses		
None	6 (23.1%)	10 (38.5%)
1-5	19 (73.1%)	15 (57.7%)
6-10	1 (3.8%)	1 (3.8%)
More than 10		

Data Collection and Data Analysis

Before the finals week, the Course Interest Survey and the Learning Outcomes and Skills Assessment scale were distributed to all students as an online survey format. All participants were allowed a week to complete both surveys. Students who attended a blended course were asked to complete an additional Delivery Mode Perceptions scale. In order to compare student learning achievement, the cumulative average for each class was calculated by the instructor and sent to the researchers.

To answer research Questions 1 to 3, independent *t*-test analyses were conducted to determine if there was a statistically significant difference in students' level of learning motivation (Research Question 1), level of learning outcomes and skills (Research Question 2),

and learning achievement (Research Question 3) between the blended and traditional courses. Descriptive analysis was conducted to answer Research Question 4.

RESULTS

Table 2 illustrates three independent *t* tests that were conducted to investigate the mean difference in students' level of motivation, level of learning outcomes and skills, and learning achievement. Students in the blended course ($M = 3.81$, $SD = .61$) reported significantly higher overall learning motivation than students in the traditional course ($M = 3.51$, $SD = .43$), $t(50) = 2.05$, $p = .045$. Among four categories of the ARCS model of motivation, a significant mean difference was found for the *Confidence* ($p = .002$) and *Satisfaction* ($p =$

TABLE 2

Independent *t* Test of Participants' Motivation, Learning Outcomes and Skills, and Learning Achievement

| | Course Delivery Format | | | |
	Blended	Traditional	*t*	*p*
Attention	3.39 (.75)	3.32 (.53)	.40	.691
Relevance	3.87 (.59)	3.58 (.53)	1.88	.066
Confidence	4.15 (.56)	3.68 (.49)	3.24	.002*
Satisfaction	3.80 (.69)	3.45 (.49)	2.12	.039*
Overall motivation	3.81 (.61)	3.51 (.43)	2.05	.045*
Learning outcomes and skills	3.79 (.73)	3.65 (.59)	.76	.450
Learning achievement (*N* = 139)	84.49 (10.19)	82.13 (10.50)	1.31	.192

.039) categories. Moreover, students in the blended course (*M* = 3.79, *SD* = .73) also reported higher levels of learning outcomes than students in the traditional course (*M* = 3.65, *SD* = .59), *t*(50) = .76, *p* = n.s. with no significant difference. With regard to students' learning achievement between the blended and traditional courses, the results of *t*-test analysis revealed that students in the blended course (*M* = 84.49, *SD* = 10.19) scored higher on their final grades than students in the traditional course (*M* = 82.13, *SD* = 10.50), *t*(137) = 1.31, *p* = n.s. with no significant difference.

This study also sought to explore students' perceptions of the blended course delivery method. The results revealed that students reported high satisfaction regarding their blended learning experience (see Table 3). They found blended classes to be more convenient because they do not have to meet in class as often (*M* = 3.92, *SD* = .80), and they would like to take more blended classes (*M* = 3.92, *SD* = .89) and would recommend blended classes to their friends (*M* = 3.92, *SD* = .89). In addition, the participants also indicated that they had adequate contact with the instructor

(*M* = 3.88, *SD* = .77) and classmates (*M* = 3.88, *SD* = .59).

DISCUSSION

This study attempted to compare the level of learning motivation, level of learning outcomes and skills, and learning achievement between students who participated in one of two different course delivery methods: blended or traditional. First, this study found significant differences on the *Confidence* and *Satisfaction* categories and overall learning motivation between the blended and traditional courses, with blended learners reporting higher levels of learning motivation. The findings confirmed that the learning content/tasks constructed and implemented in the blended learning environment are consistent with ARCS and can enhance student motivation. Blended learning enables the promotion of a flexible learning environment that reinforces the student's autonomy, reflection, and power of research (Chambers, 1999; Tam, 2000), and there is ample time for reflection on readings and online interactions with classmates during

TABLE 3
Delivery Mode Perceptions

Survey Items	Mean	SD
I had adequate contact with the instructor.	3.88	.77
I had adequate contact with my classmates.	3.88	.59
I had too many technical problems associated with this class.*	2.85	1.08
This class was more difficult than a face-to-face class.*	3.19	1.13
The flexibility of blended classes allows me to complete assignments on my own time.	3.76	.91
The quality of blended classes is NOT as good as face-to-face classes.*	2.81	.98
Blended classes are more convenient because I do not have to meet in class as often.	3.92	.80
I would like to take more blended classes.	3.92	.89
I would recommend blended classes to my friends.	3.92	.89

Note. *Reverse coded; reposes ranged from 1 (*strongly disagree*) to 5 (*strongly agree*).

online work time. For instance, using technologies (e.g., blogs, journals, and discussion boards) in a learning management system can increase opportunities for students to receive diverse opinions and feedback from classmates and the instructor. This kind of asynchronous communication and reflection is no longer limited by in-class time constraints and can be ongoing as long as there are new inputs. Ho, Lu, and Thurmaier concluded in a 2006 study that additional modes of communication and participation can lead to an increase in student motivation. Thus, students are the center of their own learning and they develop capabilities for self-directed learning and problem solving. If students have a higher level of independence in the learning process, it can help them to build confidence and satisfaction. In this case, blended learning provides a platform for forming a learning society and for building dimensions of relationships between students and the other aspects of their learning experience. According to Aspden and Helm (2004), an important part of the educational process is to build strong relationships on connection between students and the various elements of their learning experience. With the assistance of technologies, the blended learning environment has potential benefits on promoting extended time communication, learner-instructor and learner-learner interactions, and

timely feedback that can lead to strong cognitive learning. Thus, learning becomes more meaningful and learners have opportunities to synthesize different information together that promotes higher order thinking skills (Sayed, 2013). Interestingly, the results of the present study showed that there was only a slight mean difference on the *Attention* category between blended course ($M = 3.39, SD = .75$) and traditional course ($M = 3.32, SD = .53$). A plausible explanation would be that the same instructor taught both blended and traditional sections and courses content/subjects could be presented in similar ways.

With respect to the second research question, higher levels of learning outcomes and skills were found from the students in the blended learning environment. Blended learners indicated that their writing, analytical, interpersonal, and computer skills had improved as a result of this course. Additionally, although no significant difference was found in final grades, students in the blended course achieved higher performance than students in the traditional course. This result is in line with those reported by Al-Qahtani and Higgins (2013), Melton et al. (2009), and Twigg (2003). Song, Singleton, Hill, and Koh (2004) concluded that the need for social connection and learning motivation affect the success of an online learning experience. A significant relationship also had been found between learning motivation and achievement in blended learning environment in López-Pérez, Pérez-López, and Rodríguez-Ariza's (2011) and Méndez and González's (2011) studies. Learners in the 21st century desire the opportunity to learn using digitally rich curriculum and to interact using web-communication and Web 2.0 technologies. Blended learners are required to change learning environments, to interact with various formats of learning content, and to adapt different modes of communication. Therefore, self-regulation, self-motivation, and time management become critical factors for success in BL.

In terms of students' perceptions of blended courses, they were satisfied with the blended course delivery method because of its flexibility and convenience (Rovai & Jordan, 2004; Voci & Young, 2001). A blended learning environment can help students develop a higher degree of self-regulation and it allows students to make more efficient use of their time by engaging in course content and assignments when they are not attending on-campus classes. Furthermore, the participants in this study were satisfied with adequate contact with the instructor and their classmates. They were also willing to take more blended courses and indicated that they would recommend blended courses to their friends.

CONCLUSION AND SUGGESTIONS FOR FURTHER RESEARCH

This study compared and assessed students' experiences and perceptions in a blended and a traditional course, as well as their level of learning motivation, level of learning outcomes and skills, and learning achievement. The results revealed that students in the blended course reported significantly higher overall learning motivation than students in the traditional course. They also reported higher levels of learning outcomes and final grades with no significant difference. In addition, blended learners indicated that they had posi-

tive blended learning experience and would like to take more blended classes and would recommend them to their friends. Findings from the present study offer significant new insights on learning motivation in the blended learning environment and extend the implications of ARCS model among different delivery methods.

It is necessary to further investigate design specifications and course implementations between blended and traditional courses. Instructors and instructional designers need to make sure course components (learning objectives, activities, and assessments, etc.) are well structured and meaningfully connected with each other in BL environments. Moreover, out-of-class (virtual) activities should not only be designed to extend student's learning participations but to foster individualized learning based on their own particular learning needs. In addition, there is need to examine the effectiveness of pedagogical approaches on course design and to investigate its impacts on students' learning motivation and achievement. Future study is also encouraged to examine students' progression of learning motivation and learning achievement using pretest-posttest designs and to examine the relationship between learning motivation and learning achievement.

REFERENCES

Al-Qahtani, A. A., & Higgins, S. E. (2013). Effects of traditional, blended and e-learning on students' achievement in higher education. *Journal of Computer Assisted Learning, 29,* 220–234. doi:10.1111/j.1365-2729.2012.00490.x

Al-Khanjari, Z. A. (2014). Applying online learning in software engineering education. In L. Yu (Ed.), *Overcoming challenges in software engineering education: Delivering non-technical knowledge and skills* (pp. 460–473). Hershey, PA: Engineering Science Reference. doi:10.4018/978-1-4666-5800-4.ch024

Ames, C., & Archer, J. (1988). Achievement goals in the classroom: Student learning strategies and motivation processes. *Journal of Educational Psychology, 80,* 260–267.

Aspden, L., & Helm, P. (2004). Making the connection in a blended learning environment. *Educational Media International, 41*, 245–252.

Bielawski, L., & Metcalf, D. (2003). *Blended elearning: Integrating knowledge, performance support, and online learning*. Amherst, MA: HRD.

Bonk, C. J., & Graham, C. R. (2006). *The handbook of blended learning: Global perspectives, local designs*. San Francisco, CA: Pfeiffer.

Chambers, M. (1999). The efficacy and ethics of using digital multimedia for educational purposes. In A. Tait & R. Mills (Eds.), *The convergence of distance and conventional education* (pp. 5–17). London, England: Routledge.

Chen, C. C., & Jones, K. T. (2007). Blended learning vs. traditional classroom settings: Assessing effectiveness and student perceptions in an MBA accounting course. *Journal of Educators Online, 4*(1), 1–15.

Cho, M. -H., & Cho, Y. (2014). Instructor scaffolding for interaction and students' academic engagement in online learning: Mediating role of perceived online class goal structures. *The Internet and Higher Education, 21*, 25–30.

Clayton, K., Blumberg, F., & Auld, D. P. (2010). The relationship between motivation, learning strategies and choice of environment whether traditional or including an online component. *British Journal of Educational Technology, 41*, 349-364. doi:10.1111/j.1467-8535.2009.00993.x

Downes, S. (2005, October). E-learning 2.0. *ACM eLearn magazine*. Retrieved from http://elearnmag.acm.org/featured.cfm?aid=1104968

Driscoll, M. (2002). Blended learning: Let's get beyond the hype. Retrieved from https://www-07.ibm.com/services/pdf/blended_learning.pdf

Gabrielle, D. M. (2003). *The effects of technology-mediated instructional strategies on motivation, performance, and self-directed learning* (Doctoral dissertation). The Florida State University, Tallahassee, FL.

Halverson, L. R., Graham, C. R., Spring, K. J., & Drysdale, J. S. (2012). An analysis of high impact scholarship and publication trends in blended learning. *Distance Education, 33*(3), 381–413.

Heinze, A., & Procter, C. (2004). *Reflections on the use of blended learning*. Proceedings of Education in a Changing Environment, University of Salford, Education Development Unit.

Ho, A., Lu, L., & Thurmaier, K. (2006). Testing the reluctant professor's hypothesis: Evaluating a blended-learning approach to distance education. *Journal of Public Affairs Education, 12*(1), 81–102.

Keller, J. M. (1987a). Strategies for stimulating the motivation to learn. *Performance & Instruction, 26*(8), 1–7.

Keller, J. M. (1987b). The systematic process of motivational design. *Performance & Instruction, 26*(9), 1–8.

Keller, J. M., & Subhiyah, R. (1993). *Course interest survey*. Tallahassee, FL: Florida State University.

Kim, C. M., & Keller, J. M. (2008). Effects of motivational and volitional email messages (MVEM) with personal messages on undergraduate students' motivation, study habits and achievement. *British Journal of Educational Technology, 39*(1), 36–51.

Lim, D. O., & Morris, M. L. (2009). Learner and instructional factors influencing learning outcomes within a blended learning environment. *Educational Technology & Society, 12*(4), 283–293.

López-Pérez, M. V., Pérez-López, M. C., & Rodríguez-Ariza, L. (2011). Blended learning in higher education: Students' perceptions and their relation to outcomes. *Computers & Education, 56*(3), 818–826.

Means, T. B., Jonassen, D. H., & Dwyer, F. M. (1997). Enhancing relevance: Embedded ARCS strategies vs. purpose. *Educational Technology Research and Development, 45*(1), 5–17.

Meece, J., Blumenfeld, P., & Hoyle, R. (1988). Students' goal orientations and cognitive engagement in classroom activities. *Journal of Educational Psychology, 80*, 514–523.

Melton, B., Graf, H., & Chopak-Foss, J. (2009). Achievement and satisfaction in blended learning versus traditional general health course designs. *International Journal for the Scholarship of Teaching and Learning, 3*(1), 1–13.

Méndez, J. A., & González, E. J. (2011). Implementing motivational features in reactive blended learning: Application to an introductory control engineering course. *IEEE Transactions on Education, 54*(4), 619–627.

Norberg, A., Dziuban, C. D., & Moskal, P. D. (2011). A time-based blended learning model. *On the Horizon, 19*(3), 207–216.

Osguthorpe, T. R., & Graham, R. C. (2003). Blended learning environments. *Quarterly Review of Distance Education, 4*(3), 227–233.

Riffell, S., & Sibley, D. (2005). Using web-based instruction to improve large undergraduate biology courses: An evaluation of a hybrid course format. *Computers & Education, 44,* 217–235.

Rovai, A. P., & Downey, J. R. (2010). Why some distance education programs fail while others succeed in a global environment. *Internet and Higher Education, 13,* 141–147.

Rovai, A., & Jordan, H. (2004). Blended learning and sense of community: A comparative analysis with traditional and fully online graduate courses. *The International Review of Research in Open and Distance Learning, 5*(2), 1–12.

Saeed, N., Yang, Y., & Sinnappan, S. (2009). Emerging Web technologies in higher education: A case of incorporating blogs, podcasts and social bookmarks in a web programming course based on students' learning styles and technology preferences. *Educational Technology & Society, 12*(4), 98–109.

Sayed, M. (2013). Blended learning environments: The effectiveness in developing concepts and thinking skills. *Journal of Education and Practice, 4*(25), 12–17.

So, H.-J., & Brush, T. A. (2008). Student perceptions of collaborative learning, social presence and satisfaction in a blended learning environment: Relationships and critical factors. *Computers & Education, 51,* 318–336.

Song, L., Singleton, E. S., Hill, J. R., & Koh, M. H. (2004). Improving online learning: Student perceptions of useful and challenging characteristic. *Internet and Higher Education, 7,* 59–70.

Sydnor, S., Sass, M., Adeola, M., & Snuggs, T. (2014), Qualitative analysis of multidisciplinary college students in an international alternative break course. *The Online Journal of Quality in Higher Education, 1*(1), 27–34.

Tam, M. (2000). Constructivism, instructional design, and technology: Implications for transforming distance learning. *Educational Technology and Society, 3*(2), 50–60.

Twigg, C. A. (2003). Improving learning and reducing costs: New models for online learning. *EDUCAUSE Review, 38*(5), 29–38.

Voci, E., & Young, K. (2001). Blended learning working in a leadership development programme. *Industrial and Commercial Training, 37*(55), 157–161.

Woo, Y., & Reeves, T. (2007). Meaningful interaction in web-based learning: A social constructivist interpretation. *Internet and Higher Education, 10,* 15–25. doi:10.1016/j.iheduc.2006.10.005

CONFERENCE CALENDAR

Charles Schlosser
Nova Southeastern University

The following conferences may be of interest to the readers of the *Quarterly Review of Distance Education.*

Distance Teaching and Learning Conference, August 9-11, Madison, WI

"The Annual Conference on Distance Teaching & Learning is recognized internationally for its quality, integrity, and longevity. For more than 30 years the premier conference in distance education has welcomed thousands of speakers and distance education and training professionals to share ideas, resources, research, and best practices."
https://dtlconference.wisc.edu/

AECT International Convention, October 17-21, Las Vegas, NV

"The AECT International Convention brings together participants from around the world offering practical applications, cutting-edge research, hands-on workshops, and demonstrations of the newest technologies and teaching/learning techniques in the field. Take this opportunity to connect with your peers at the 2016 convention in Las Vegas!"
http://www.aect.org/events/call/

E-Learn 2016: World Conference on E-Learning, November 14-16, Washington, DC

"This annual conference serves as a multidisciplinary forum for the exchange of information on research, development, and applications of all topics related to e-Learning in the corporate, government, healthcare, and higher education sectors."
https://www.aace.org/conf/elearn/

OLC Accelerate, November 16-18, Orlando, FL

"OLC Accelerate is the new name of the Annual Online Learning Consortium International Conference, now in its 22nd year. We chose OLC Accelerate because this conference is devoted to driving quality online learning, advancing best practice guidance and accelerating innovation in learning for academic leaders, educators, administrators, online learning professionals and organizations around the world."

• **Charles Schlosser**, Associate Program Professor, Nova Southeastern University, 1750 NE 167 St., North Miami Beach, FL 33162. E-mail: charles.schlosser@nova.edu

---

The Quarterly Review of Distance Education, Volume 17(1), 2016, pp. 53–54
Copyright © 2016 Information Age Publishing, Inc.
ISSN 1528-3518

http://onlinelearningconsortium.org/olc-accelerate/

FETC, January 24-27, 2017, Orlando, FL

"The Future of Education Technology Conference offers unparalleled opportunities to explore the evolving role of technology in the enhancement of learning and improvement of performance in pre-K–12 schools and districts. FETC brings together a collaborative community of educational leaders and technology experts to exchange techniques and empower participants with strategies for teaching and learning success."
http://fetc.org

AUTHOR BIOGRAPHICAL DATA

Bruce A. Cameron is an associate professor of family and consumer sciences at the University of Wyoming in the Textiles and Merchandising program area and is the department chair. Cameron has been teaching online classes since 2002 at the undergraduate level. His research interests include teaching in an online setting, particularly student and faculty perceptions of group work, the evaluation of the effectiveness of domestic laundry detergents, and the yellowing propensity of U.S. wool.

Michelle Moore, a former middle school math teacher, has been an advocate for Moodle since finding it more than 10 years ago during a review of learning management systems while completing her master's degree in instructional design and technology. Enamored with Moodle's capabilities and its foundation in social constructionism, it was not long before Moore's passion led her to a full-time position training and providing support for educators and trainers in schools, universities, and businesses across North America. Michelle is pursuing a doctorate in learning technologies at University of North Texas where she is actively researching online education and constructivist teaching methods.

Kari Morgan is an associate professor of family studies and human services at Kansas State University and is the coordinator of the undergraduate program in family studies and human services and the director of assessment for the College of Human Ecology. Morgan's research interests focus on issues and challenges facing rural families, and the scholarship of teaching and learning. Morgan's first experience with distance teaching was as a graduate student at the University of Wisconsin-Madison, where she assisted with telecourse delivery of a child development course. She currently teaches courses in both online and face-to-face formats.

Alana S. Phillips's current research interests involve various aspects of online instruction and teacher education. She recently completed her PhD in learning technologies at the University of North Texas and plans to use her education to help K–12 students and teachers. She is a former middle school language arts and Texas history teacher. Prior to starting her K–12 career, she served 21 years as a U.S. Army officer, working in both human resources and systems automation.

Heather Robinson is a PhD candidate in learning technologies at the University of North Texas in the College of Information. She is an instructor for courses in the program areas of computer science, computer information systems and learning technologies for Casper College and the University of North Texas. Robinson has presented and is published on her research on constructivist online learning, instructional design, learning communities, student technology proficiency, and faculty experiences with online technology

The Quarterly Review of Distance Education, Volume 17(1), 2016, pp. 55–56
Copyright © 2016 Information Age Publishing, Inc.

ISSN 1528-3518

adoption. She earned her master's degree in information science from the University of North Texas. Prior to her work in academia, Heather worked in information technology as a computer consultant and trainer.

Mapopa William Sanga obtained his PhD in instructional design and technology at Virginia Tech in 2011. Since 2013, he has been working as an assistant professor and teaching and learning coordinator at Southwestern Oklahoma State University in the United States.

Anneliese Sheffield's research interests include online learning and the impact of technology use on human interactions and relationships. Anneliese is a doctoral candidate in the Department of Learning Technologies at the University of North Texas. Her interest in online learning stems from personal experience as an online student living around the world. Anneliese has presented and published on constructivist online learning, digital storytelling, and parent-child cogaming.

Hungwei Tseng is an instructional designer in the Office of Teaching, Learning, & Technology and an assistant professor in the Department of Educational Resources at Jacksonville State University. His research interests include distance learning, online group development, problem-based instruction, blended learning, and innovative learning technologies.

Christine E. Wade is an associate professor of family and consumer sciences at the University of Wyoming in the Human Development and Family Sciences program area. Her research interests include after-school programming, positive youth development, and the scholarship of teaching. Wade has taught both graduate and undergraduate courses using online technology.

Eamonn Joseph Walsh, Jr. serves as the associate vice president in the Office of Teaching, Learning, & Technology at Jacksonville State University where he oversees the integration and support of online and blended instruction and faculty development.

Lynette Watts has been an assistant professor with Midwestern State University for 12 years. She has taught radiology professional students in the bachelor of science, radiologic technology and bachelor of science, radiologic science programs and is currently teaching in the master of science, radiologic science program. Her research interests focus on best practices in distance education such as student engagement, cyberbullying prevention, and academic integrity. Watts resides in Wichita Falls with her husband, Air Force MSgt (Ret) Roger "Gar" Watts and their two dachshund-mix dogs, Theo and Freddie.

Karen C. Williams is a professor emeritus of family and consumer sciences at the University of Wyoming and is the director of the online Bachelors of Applied Sciences degree programs. Williams has been teaching using distance methodologies her entire career, and was responsible for the development of the department's online bachelor's degree program in child development, which began in 1999. In 2011, she was the recipient of the University of Wyoming's inaugural Technology Instructional Enhancement Fellowship. Her research interests include preservice preparation of early childhood educators, distance education, and multiculturalism and diversity issues.